How to Pass
THE POLICE INITIAL RECRUITMENT TEST

D1079864

35104

How to Pass
THE POLICE INITIAL
RECRUITMENT TEST

**Ken Thomas, Catherine Tolley
and Harry Tolley**

**KOGAN
PAGE**

First published in 1997

Apart from any fair dealing for the purposes of research or private study, or criticism or review, as permitted under the Copyright, Designs and Patents Act, 1988, this publication may only be reproduced, stored or transmitted, in any form or by any means, with the prior permission in writing of the publishers, or in the case of reprographic reproduction in accordance with the terms and licences issued by the CLA. Enquiries concerning reproduction outside those terms should be sent to the publishers at the undermentioned address:
Kogan Page Limited
120 Pentonville Road
London N1 9JN

© Harry Tolley, Ken Thomas and Cath Tolley 1997

The right of Harry Tolley, Ken Thomas and Cath Tolley to be identified as the authors of this work has been asserted by them in accordance with the Copyright, Designs and Patents Act 1988.

British Library Cataloguing in Publication Data
A CIP record for this book is available from the British Library.

ISBN 0–7494–21347

Typeset by Florencetype Ltd, Stoodleigh, Devon

Printed and bound in Great Britain by
Biddles Ltd, Guildford and Kings Lynn

Contents

Introduction

Most people think that they know a lot about police work. During our everyday lives we observe police officers carrying out their duties, and through television news, documentary and drama programmes we gain further insights into many aspects of policing. The accuracy of the information gained in this way will vary depending on the circumstances in which we come into contact with the police, and the nature of the programmes we watch on television. With regard to the latter there is a tendency to both sensationalise and glamorise in ways that can give us unrealistic impressions of the work and lives of police officers. However, whether or not you have a realistic idea of the nature of policing, this is likely to be one of the topics on which your knowledge and understanding will be assessed during the selection process. The precise details of the procedures used in that process vary from force to force, but one element which they have in common is the Police Initial Recruitment Test (PIRT).

The PIRT consists of five individually timed sub tests which have been designed to measure the candidates' competence in the core skills they will need if they are to become effective police officers. These are:

- PIR 1 Verbal Usage, which assesses the written communication skills needed to make notes, take statements and write reports.
- PIR 2 Checking, which assesses the clerical checking skills needed to recognise errors in documents and computer-held records.
- PIR 3 Numerical Reasoning, which assesses the numeracy skills needed to carry out arithmetic calculations and interpret statistical data.
- PIR 4 Verbal Logical Reasoning, which assesses the logical reasoning skills needed to evaluate evidence, make deductions and draw conclusions.

● PIR 5 Observation, which assesses the observation skills needed to recall information about incidents which have been witnessed in everyday settings.

In order to help you to prepare for the PIRT, approximately two thirds of this book consists of practice tests which are similar to four of the sub tests (PIR1–PIR4) that make up the complete test. Because it is based on a video recording, it has not been possible to provide practice tests in this book for the fifth sub test – ie, PIR5 Observation. However, in Chapter 8 we give detailed guidance on what to expect in the real PIRT, and suggest various ways in which you can prepare for it. You will find the answers to the practice tests at the end of each chapter.

The practice tests in this book have arisen from work which the authors have done with employers such as the Police and the Civil Service. The tests have been piloted and our evaluation studies have demonstrated that regular use of practice tests such as these can improve a candidate's performance significantly. Experience also shows that doing well on a test is not only a question of aptitude and intelligence, but also a matter of determination and self-confidence. Our research shows that regular use of practice tests can help to boost the candidates' self-confidence, and enable them to cope with the nervousness and stress they experience when taking tests as important as the PIRT.

The systematic use of the practice tests provided here should help you in the following ways:

● to become familiar with the different subtests in the PIRT;
● to learn to work more effectively under the time pressures you will experience under test conditions;
● to improve your test techniques so that you do not lose marks through simple errors.

The continuous feedback you will receive as you work through the tests should help to boost your self-confidence. This in turn should help to reduce your anxiety and prevent you from panicking when confronted with the PIRT.

However, in order to succeed you will need to be well motivated, to take practice seriously and to work hard on any weaknesses which become apparent in your practice test results. If you experience serious difficulty in coping with the tests it does not mean that you are a failure and that you will never be able to succeed. It simply means that the practice tests have helped you to identify a problem which you must address before you can make further progress. It is much better to discover these through practice tests (when you still have time to do something about them) than finding out from the result of your PIRT!

It is also very important to recognise that the PIRT is just one element in the selection process. Passing this test does not mean that you will be offered an appointment. In fact there is a strong possibility that more candidates will pass the PIRT than the number of vacancies available. This means that if you are really serious about becoming a police officer, you must give some thought to the other methods used by the force to which you have applied to select new recruits. In order to succeed in one force, for example, you would have to clear each of the assessment 'hurdles' shown in Figure 1.

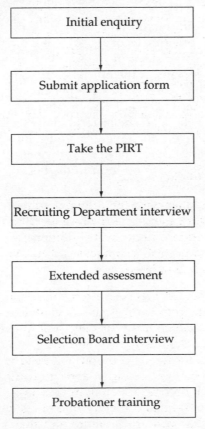

Figure 1 Assessment hurdles in the selection process

Unfortunately, many candidates are unsuccessful because they fail to demonstrate their true potential as a result of:

- anxiety and stress;
- having to complete the PIRT quickly and accurately under test conditions;
- poor test techniques;
- having to perform in front of other people while being observed and evaluated;
- not knowing what skills are being assessed.

Careful and systematic preparation for the whole selection process, including the use of practice tests such as the ones provided here, can help to overcome the causes of failure as listed above, and in so doing to avoid the sense of disappointment and frustrated ambition which follows.

The purpose of this book, therefore, is to offer guidance to would-be police officers on how to prepare themselves for the PIRT and for the other types of assessment which they are likely to encounter at some stage in the selection process. We begin in Chapter 1 by looking at the official entry requirements which they must all satisfy, as well as the personal qualities that are sought in potential police officers. In Chapter 2 we give guidance on some of the assessment techniques which are used by police forces to select their new recruits. Information on the ways in which practice can have a positive effect on your PIRT results by helping you to perform to the best of your ability, is provided in Chapter 3.

Chapter 1

Entry Requirements and Personal Qualities

The aim of this chapter is to provide you with guidance on the entry requirements for the police service and the skills and abilities sought in potential police officers. This should help you to understand the qualities that you will be expected to display at different stages in the selection process.

Entry requirements

There is, at present, no national police service. Instead, there are 43 separate police forces covering the whole of England and Wales. All forces are run independently under the command of a Chief Officer who is responsible for the control of the force and the policing of the area. Each force recruits independently, a consequence of which is that entry requirements vary slightly from one force to another, so the following summary provides only general guidance. For further information, you should write to the Chief Officer of the force you would like to join. Graduates interested in the Accelerated Promotion Scheme should first write to the Graduate Liaison Officer, Police Department, Home Office, Queen Anne's Gate, London, SW1H 9AT.

- The minimum age for appointment as a constable is 18½ years. There is no upper age limit except for the graduate Accelerated Promotion Scheme for which the upper age limit is 30.
- Applicants must meet the nationality requirement by being either British citizens, or Commonwealth citizens whose stay in the UK is not subject to restrictions, or citizens of the Irish Republic.
- Applicants should have a good standard of education. Most forces will require candidates to take the PIRT. However, if you have four GCSEs (or equivalent) at grades A to C, which

include English Language and Maths, then you may be exempt from taking the test. A degree is required for the Accelerated Promotion Scheme.

● You must be in good health and have a good physique. All candidates have to pass a full medical examination before they can be appointed.

● All forces require a high standard of eyesight; some forces' requirements are higher than others. No force can accept you if you have only one eye, cannot distinguish the principal colours (red, green or violet), or if you suffer from squint or other eye conditions which are liable to the risk of aggravation or recurrence. Most, but not all, forces will accept you if you wear contact lenses or glasses.

● There are no minimum or maximum height requirements.

● The police are equal opportunities employers, and particularly welcome applications from women and from ethnic minority groups.

Personal qualities

Police work is not like any other occupation. When, as a police officer, you are out on patrol, whether on foot or in a car, you will never know what you might be required to do next. It could be, for example, that you have to give directions to a tourist, deal with a lost child, attend a road accident, give evidence in court, or even confront a dangerous criminal. The list of tasks that you could be required to undertake is almost endless and this makes the work of police officers both interesting and demanding. It is work that requires physical, mental and moral courage, intelligence, flexibility, knowledge and a sense of values.

These personal qualities form the basis of the skills and abilities which Probationer Training aims to develop in new recruits. The selection process, therefore, is intended to assess your potential to achieve acceptable standards in each of the categories set out in the checklist given below. A good starting point, therefore, in your preparation for selection would be to use the checklist to carry out a self-assessment. This should provide you with a broad indication of your strengths and weaknesses in relation to those personal qualities which are relevant to the work of police officers. You will then be able to build on those strengths and work on your weakness in order to improve your chances of success in the selection process. When completing the checklist, you should keep in mind that people are rarely exclusively one thing or another. So, if you agree more than you disagree with a statement, circle 'Yes'. On the other hand, if you disagree more than you agree with a statement, then you should circle 'No'.

1. Desired character traits

These are the human characteristics or attitudes that all successful candidates will be expected to possess. Although it is possible to bring about changes in this area, it is recognised that change is unlikely to be achieved through the initial training process. Deficiencies in this area are, then, likely to be regarded as serious weaknesses. It will be to your advantage therefore, to identify any particular weaknesses and to begin working on them as soon as possible.

I recognise the importance of being punctual and
strive to complete work on time.   Yes/No
I take pride in my appearance.   Yes/No
I am reliable and can be trusted to complete work
without supervision.   Yes/No
I concentrate on what is being done or said and am
not easily distracted.   Yes/No
I have moral principles and physical courage.   Yes/No
I can use my imagination to approach problems in
a creative way.   Yes/No
I am self-motivated and have an active interest in
police work and a wide range of other activities.   Yes/No
I have helpful and considerate attitudes to others
and am prepared to put the needs of others before
my own.   Yes/No
I am responsible, trustworthy, honest and loyal.   Yes/No

2. Monitoring personal performance

Probationer training involves a good deal of self-assessment and this category is concerned with skills of self-observation, self-regulation and taking the appropriate action.

I am capable of monitoring my own performance
through personal reflection and feedback from
others.   Yes/No

I understand the symptoms and causes of stress
and am sensitive to the needs of others who may
be under stress.   Yes/No
I am capable of reaching the required standard of
physical fitness.   Yes/No
I recognise the importance of learning from
experience and draw on past experiences to deal
with the situation in hand.   Yes/No

3. Communication and relationships with others

This category includes the skills that police officers need when
talking to people, whether they are victims, witnesses, offenders
or other members of the public.

When dealing with other people I give proper
consideration to their feelings.   Yes/No
I have a basic understanding of how my body
language can influence how others interpret what
I am saying.   Yes/No
I have good oral communication skills and can
present reports in a clear and concise manner.   Yes/No
I listen carefully to what is being said and am
prepared to ask questions for clarification when
necessary.   Yes/No
I have good self-control and am tolerant of the
views and behaviour of others even when provoked.   Yes/No
I understand that there are legal limitations on use
of physical force.   Yes/No
I can establish good relationships with others,
accept proper discipline and be a good team member. Yes/No

4. Investigation

Investigating crime is obviously a fundamental part of the duties
of a police officer. This category covers the skills that are
employed when police officers are trying to discover why and
by whom a particular act was committed.

I can assess situations with an open and enquiring
mind, and tackle problems from different angles.   Yes/No
I can structure a series of questions which will elicit
relevant information.   Yes/No

I can collate and analyse information in ways that
will enable relevant information to be identified. Yes/No

5. Knowledge

Knowledge of the law, police equipment and procedures, and
the local community are clearly very important. Much of this
knowledge will be developed in Probationer Training. What we
are concerned with here is providing you with an indication of
your potential for success in such training.

I understand the importance of taking personal
responsibility for developing my knowledge of
the law. Yes/No
I am capable of developing a knowledge of the
technical skills needed to use police operational
equipment. Yes/No
I understand that it is necessary to have a knowledge
of the policies and guidelines which govern police
procedures. Yes/No
I recognise the importance of community awareness
and the perceptions the community have of the
police. Yes/No

6. Decision making

This category is concerned with those situations where police
officers are confronted with a situation, such as a dispute, where
they have to make decisions and solve problems there and then.

I can identify a problem and make a decision when
presented with alternative solutions. Yes/No
I can set objectives in relation to priorities and plan
my work accordingly Yes/No
I am flexible and can modify decisions in the light
of new information. Yes/No
I understand the importance of obtaining a clear
understanding of both sides of the problem when
dealing with conflict and ambiguity. Yes/No

7. Practical effectiveness

Having made a decision, or solved a problem, or simply discovered some facts, police officers need confidence to carry out their decisions in practice. Once they have done this, they need to be able to take responsibility for what they have done. This category is concerned with getting on and doing things.

I am capable of taking the initiative in circumstances where this is required.	Yes/No
I have confidence in my ability to handle a wide range of tasks.	Yes/No
I am prepared to take responsibility for my own decisions and actions.	Yes/No
I am capable of exercising leadership and giving appropriate directions to others.	Yes/No

8. Written reports

This is clearly an important area as most police work requires officers to write something down, whether it is a Crime Report, a statement or simply a message.

I can take clear and accurate notes and know how to use them to write intelligible and factually correct reports.	Yes/No

In carrying out such a personal audit at this stage, it is important to remember that what you are trying to do is to evaluate your potential to achieve, with training and support, the levels of competence set out in the checklist. When you have completed the audit, you could ask someone who knows you well and whose opinions you trust, to cross-check your assessments. This will help to ensure that you have identified accurately your main strengths and weaknesses which you should summarise in the spaces in the box below. With this knowledge you will be able to develop an action plan to build on your strengths and address your weaknesses.

The strengths on which I can build are:

The weaknesses I need to address are:

For further guidance on assessing your potential for different types of employment, we recommend that you consult one of the other books in this series – for example, *Test Your Own Aptitude* (Barrett and Williams).

Chapter 2

How Skills and Abilities are Assessed

The aim of this chapter is to help you to understand how the skills and abilities outlined in Chapter 1 are assessed in the police selection process.

Extended assessment

It is now widely recognised that an interview is an unreliable method of assessing a candidate's suitability for most types of employment. In consequence, employers use a variety of methods, including interviews, in order to assess the capabilities of potential employees. Standardised tests are another commonly used technique. However, success in a test such as the PIRT will only establish that a candidate satisfies what might be regarded as the 'base line' requirements for the job. As we pointed out in the Introduction, the chances are that far more candidates will be successful in the PIRT than the number of vacancies available at any one time. Consequently, a police force may ask those candidates who have achieved a satisfactory score on the PIRT to take additional tests in order to find out more about them. You can prepare yourself for this eventuality by referring to other titles in this series, including: *How to Pass Verbal Reasoning Tests* and *How to Pass Numeracy Tests* (both by Tolley and Thomas).

In order to conduct a thorough and reliable assessment of the potential of applicants, the police, like many other employers, observe and assess the performance of applicants on a variety of individual and group tasks. Because this takes place over a period of time and involves the use of different techniques, it is often referred to as 'extended assessment'. Details of the way in which such assessments are conducted will vary from force to force, but the following notes for guidance should help you to understand and appreciate the principles behind:

- the assessment criteria which may be used;
- how extended assessment may be structured;
- the assessment exercises candidates may be asked to do.

Assessment criteria

The following criteria were used by officers in the Recruiting Department of one force to evaluate the performance of applicants during an extended assessment which we observed:

- **Smartness**: The degree to which the candidate impresses with his/her appearance.
- **Bearing**: Disregarding the standard of dress, how does the candidate 'carry' himself/herself? For example, how does he/she stand and does he/she slouch in the chair?
- **Oral skills**: Can the candidate put over his/her thoughts in a clear and understandable way?
- **Writing skills**: Can the candidate communicate clearly and accurately in writing?
- **Self-confidence**: Could the candidate face up to typical policing situations and tasks now or in the future with appropriate training?
- **Impact**: Has the candidate sufficient 'presence', either through personality or oral skills, to impose his/her will when required?
- **Leadership**: Would the candidate be able to display appropriate situational control as a police officer now or in the future with appropriate training?
- **Attitude towards others**: Can the candidate talk to and work with others without confrontation or upset? Does he/she display any evidence of prejudices that would make him/her unacceptable?
- **Empathy**: Does the candidate show consideration for the feelings of others? Is there any evidence that he/she is tactless and insensitive?
- **Sense of humour**: Has the candidate the ability to laugh at himself/herself and use appropriate humour to reduce tension and aggression?
- **Initiative**: Does the candidate show skills and enthusiasm in dealing with new situations or problems?
- **Depth of thought**: Has the candidate the ability to understand and develop a topic being discussed?

- **Police knowledge/awareness**: Has the candidate fully thought about her/his application? Has he/she a realistic appreciation of police work? Has he/she taken the opportunity to speak to serving police officers?
- **Current affairs**: Has the candidate a reasonable knowledge and interest in the world about him/her?

Assessment programme

The length of time over which extended assessment is carried out will vary from force to force, as will the range of activities included in the assessment programme. However, the account given below should give you a reasonable idea of what to expect in terms of the types of activities which may be used and the attributes they are intended to assess.

This particular programme was conducted over an evening and the whole of the following day. Candidates assembled on the first evening to take a physical fitness test. This includes tests of strength, stamina and speed and you should find out what the standards you will be expected to achieve are, in order to prepare yourself for them. However, if you do not take regular exercise already, you should seek advice (including consulting your doctor) before you embark on a fitness training programme.

If you are required to attend an assessment that requires an overnight stay, you must remember that you are being assessed continuously. Police officers are police officers 24 hours a day, and inappropriate behaviour during 'free time' will not be overlooked simply because you are not engaged on a formal activity.

As the candidates work through the exercises which make up the programme for the second day, the assessors will gradually build up an individual profile of each candidate, covering the assessment criteria itemised above. An example of a programme for a day of extended assessment is given below.

0900–0910	Opening address by senior Recruiting Officer
0910–0930	Autobiographies
0930–0945	Group discussion
0945–1030	Group logical reasoning exercise
1030–1045	Break

1045–1200	Statement taking
1200–1245	General knowledge and current affairs test
1245–1345	Break
1345–1430	Lecturettes
1430–1500	Problem-solving test
1500–1630	Individual interview/debriefing
1630	Dispersal

Assessment exercises

The programme given above provides examples of the main types of assessment exercise which may be used in addition to pencil and paper tests during extended assessment. The account which follows of sample exercises is intended to gives you an idea of what to expect, and to show how they are related to the assessment criteria outlined above.

Autobiographies

In this exercise candidates are allocated to groups of about ten. Each candidate is then required to stand in front of the group and is allowed two minutes to tell the group something of interest about himself/herself. This exercise, often used as an 'ice-breaker', can clearly be quite stressful. This is particularly so if the candidate has little or no experience of making presentations. As many of the extended assessment activities require the public expression of thoughts and ideas, this is an essential skill that needs to be developed. In addition, an initial assessment will also be made of the candidate's smartness, bearing, self-confidence, and sense of humour.

Group discussion

A common exercise in extended assessment is a 'leaderless' group discussion. The assessors provide a topic for discussion and then observe candidates as the debate proceeds. Although the assessors may intervene to encourage some candidates to participate or to change the topic so that about four or five topics are covered in the time allowed, they take no part in the discussion. Typical discussion topics are those which encourage differing reactions and opinions to emerge – for example:

- Should we be judged by our appearance?
- Should women police officers patrol alone?
- Is there any moral difference between tax avoidance and tax evasion?
- Should the deployment of ethnic minority police officers be primarily in predominantly ethnic minority areas?
- Are race and sex discrimination overstated problems?

Observation of groups discussing topics such as these enable assessors to make judgements about the candidate's bearing, oral skills, self-confidence, impact, leadership, attitude to others, empathy, sense of humour, initiative, depth of thought, police awareness, and knowledge of current affairs.

Group logical reasoning exercises

The purpose of this exercise is slightly different from the group discussion. Here the purpose is to examine the candidate's ability to interact and communicate within a group whose purpose is to arrive at a joint decision after assimilating various sources of information. In some of these exercises, such as 'Desert Survival', 'Lost at Sea' and 'Crisis on the Moon', each member of the group is provided with the same information about the items of equipment that survivors of an accident have been able to salvage and the environmental conditions that they are likely to experience. The group has then to come to an agreed ranking of the importance of the items of equipment to their survival in the particular environment. The group's final ranking may then be compared to the ranking given by an experienced survival expert.

Variations of this type of exercise may include, for example, such things as accounts of the movements of a group of 'villains' at the time a murder was committed. In this type of exercise it is important to begin by collating all of the information contained on the individual briefing sheets. This will not only help you in the process of eliminating those who could not have carried out the 'murder' but, more importantly, help you to ensure that the group has all of the information available to it.

It is essential, however, that you keep in mind that although these exercises have 'objective' outcomes, in that your results can be compared to those of an 'expert' or the evidence shows that only one of the 'villains' could have carried out the 'murder', the way in which the group goes about the task is possibly more important than the outcome. Observation of the ways in which candidates participate in the group process enables assessments to be made of their oral skills, logical reasoning, self-confidence, impact, leadership, attitudes towards others, empathy, sense of humour, initiative, and depth of thought.

Statement-taking exercise

In this type of exercise the candidates are asked to imagine that they are police officers who have been detailed to interview a possible 'witness' to, for example, a 'hit-and-run' road accident. They are given ten minutes to prepare the questions that will elicit the information that will enable the driver of the car to be traced. The person who plays the 'witness' will probably have been briefed to offer information only in response to direct questions. It is important, therefore, to use the preparation time to think systematically about the information you need to obtain from the witness, the questions that will elicit it, and how you will record the information during the interview. The candidates are then allowed ten minutes each to interview the witness.

In the case of such an exercise based on a hit-and-run road accident, it would be important in the interview to obtain information related to the witness, the vehicle, and the driver. Think about this for a moment and then use the spaces in the box below to jot down the information you think it would be helpful to obtain in the interview. You can then compare your ideas with the suggestions given in the box at the end of the chapter.

Witness:

Vehicle:

Driver:

Following the interviews, candidates may be allowed some time to prepare an account of what the witness has told them. In doing this they will have to rely on notes taken during the interview in order to write an accurate statement. Exercises such as this are not intended to test the ability of candidates to take and write a police 'statement', as thorough training in doing this is provided after appointment. However, the exercise does allow an assessment to be made of a candidate's abilities in a number of areas including interpersonal skills, oral skills, logical reasoning, self-confidence, planning, ability to elicit information, recall of factual data, and writing skills.

Lecturettes

In this exercise candidates are forewarned that they will be required to speak for five minutes on a topic of their choice. The assessors may in this instance create more challenging and stressful circumstances by interrupting with questions. The purpose behind such an exercise is to observe the way in which the candidates present the topic and deal with the interruptions. Assessments are then made of the candidates' presentation skills, self-confidence, sense of humour, ability to 'think on their feet', self-presentation and stress tolerance. These assessments are then used to cross-check with those made during the auto-biographical presentations.

Final thoughts

Being faced with extended assessment tasks like those outlined above, following directly on from the PIRT, will probably seem a daunting experience for most candidates. It is important to remember, therefore, that the selection process is not intended to be easy. Those who have designed it know from experience that if you cannot cope with the assessment tasks they set you during the extended assessment it very unlikely that you will cope with the demands of Probationer Training. They have a responsibility to select from the large number of applications they receive, those candidates whom they judge to have a very good chance of becoming effective and successful police officers. The work of the police service is too important for them to take that responsibility lightly.

Witness: Name, age, sex, address, alone or accompanied, approximate distance from incident, etc.

Vehicle: Saloon, estate or hatchback, colour, registration number (or part of), identifying stickers, identifying marks or damage, make.

Driver: Male/female, ethnic group, height, age, clothes, sole occupant or with passengers.

Chapter 3

How to Prepare for the PIRT

The aims of this chapter are to help you to understand how practice can have a positive effect on your PIRT results, perform under test conditions to the best of your ability, to make effective use of the practice tests in this book, and to interpret your scores.

Practice tests can make a difference

Many candidates underachieve in selection tests because they are over-anxious and because they have not known what to expect. Practice tests are designed to help you to overcome both of these common causes of failure. The practice tests provided in the later chapters of this book will help you to become familiar with four of the five subtests which make up the PIRT. Regular practice will also give you the opportunity to work under conditions similar to those which you will experience when taking the real test. In particular, they should help you to become accustomed to working under the pressure of the strict time limits which are imposed in standardised tests like the PIRT. Familiarity with the demands of the subtests and working under simulated test conditions should help you to cope better with any nervousness you might experience when taking the PIRT – that is, when the result really matters.

How to perform to the best of your ability

Our experience over many years of preparing candidates for public examinations and standardised tests leads us to suggest that if you want to perform to the best of your ability in a selection test like the PIRT you should read and act on the advice given below.

- Make sure that you know what you have to do before you start putting pencil to paper – if you do not understand, ask the person who is administering the test.
- Read the instructions carefully before each subtest starts in order to make sure that you understand. Don't skim through them – you may overlook important details and in consequence make mistakes you could have avoided.
- Even if you have taken the test before, don't assume that the instructions (and the worked examples) are the same as the last time – they may have been changed.
- Read the instructions carefully and highlight/underline the 'command words' (that is, those words which tell you what to do).
- Once the test begins work as quickly and as accurately as you can. Remember, every unanswered item is a scoring chance you have missed!
- Check frequently to make sure that the questions you have answered match the spaces you have filled in on the answer sheet.
- Avoid spending too much time on questions you find difficult – leave them and go back to them later if you have time.
- If you are uncertain about an answer, enter your best reasoned choice (but avoid simply 'guessing').
- If you have some spare time after you have answered all the questions, go back and check through your answers.
- Keep working as hard as you can throughout the test – the more correct answers you get the higher your score will be.
- Concentrate your mind on the test itself and nothing else – you cannot afford to allow yourself to be distracted.
- Be positive in your attitude. Previous failures in tests or examinations are in the past and should not be allowed to have a detrimental effect on your performance on this occasion.

How to use the practice tests

In order to derive maximum benefit from the use of practice tests, you should read and act on the advice given below. This consists of three sets of checklists to guide you through different stages – that is, *before* you begin, *during* a practice test and *after* you have completed it.

Before you attempt any of the tests make sure that you:

● have a supply of sharpened pencils, an eraser and some paper for doing rough work;
● have a clock or watch with an alarm which you can set to make sure that you work within the recommended time limits;
● are in a quiet room where you will not be disturbed or distracted, and which has an uncluttered desk/table at which you can work;
● have decided in advance which test you are going to tackle;
● have reviewed what you learned from previous practice sessions;
● have read the instructions (at the start of the relevant chapter) on how to complete the test, making sure that you understand them before you begin;
● have worked through the examples provided so that you know exactly what to do before you start;
● know how to record your answers correctly.

You should then be ready to set your timer and tackle the chosen practice test.

During the practice test itself you should try to:

● work quickly and systematically through the items – and whatever you do, don't panic;
● move on to the next question as quickly as you can if you get stuck at any point – you can always return to the unfinished items at the end if you have time to do so;
● check your answers if you have time to do so at the end;
● use spare paper for your rough work;
● stop working as soon as the time is up (and mark the point you have reached in the test if there are any items which you have not yet completed).

After the practice test you should:

● check your answers by referring to the answers given at the end of the relevant chapter;
● put a tick (✓) against each question which you answered correctly and a cross (✗) next to each one which was incorrect;
● only score as correct those questions for which you filled in exactly the right answer spaces – anything different from those given in the answer sheet should be marked incorrect;

- add up the number of ticks to give you your score on the test as a whole;
- compare your score with those on previous tests of the same type to see what progress you are making;
- work through any items which you did not manage to complete in the test and check your answers;
- try to work out where you went wrong with any questions which you answered incorrectly.

Try to talk through the methods you used to arrive at your answers with someone who has also completed the test. This will help to consolidate your learning by:

- helping you to understand why you answered certain questions incorrectly;
- giving you a better understanding of the questions which you answered correctly;
- suggesting different ways of arriving at the same answer to a question.

Discussion of this kind should also help you to reach an understanding of the principles which underpin the design and construction of a test. If you can begin to get 'inside the mind' of the person who set the questions, you will be in a much better position to answer them when required to do so in a real test. This would be an especially useful way of preparing for the PIR4 Verbal Logical Reasoning Test. Working collaboratively with another person can also help to keep you motivated and provide you with encouragement and 'moral' support if and when you need it.

Interpreting your practice test scores

Because they tend to be shorter than the real subtests in the PIRT and have not been taken under exactly the same conditions, you should not read too much into your practice test scores. You will probably find that the PIR subtests will be more exacting because they will be:

- longer in duration than the examples provided in this book;
- administered formally in a standardised way by a person who has been trained in their use;
- more stressful than practice tests.

Nevertheless, your practice test scores should provide you with some useful feedback on the following:

- how your performance on the same type of test – for example, numerical reasoning or verbal usage – has varied from one practice test to another, and hence what progress you have made over a given period of time;
- how well you have done on one type of test compared to another, and hence what your relative strengths and weaknesses seem to be.

However, when trying to make sense of your practice test scores, you should remember that in the PIRT the overall score you achieve will be compared with the performance of a group of typical candidates in order to determine how well or badly you have done.

Making use of feedback from practice tests

More important than your total score on a practice test is *how* you achieved that overall mark. For example, you could begin such an analysis by noting the answer to the following questions:

- How many questions did you attempt within the given time limit and how many remained unanswered?
- How many of the questions that you attempted did you answer correctly?
- Where in the practice test were most of your incorrect answers – for example, at the end when you were hurrying, or at the beginning before you had calmed your nerves and settled down to work?
- Were there any particular types of question which you answered incorrectly?

The answers to these questions should give you some pointers as to how you might improve your scores in future practice tests by helping you to change your behaviour – for example:

- if you got most of the questions right but left too many unanswered, you should try to work more quickly next time;
- if you managed to answer all the questions but got a lot of them wrong, then you should try to be more accurate even if this means that you have to work more slowly.

Remember, the object of the exercise in standardised tests is to score as many correct answers as you can in the time allowed. Thus, you need to strike a balance between speed and accuracy. Regular practice, careful evaluation of your performance and intelligent use of feedback can help to get the balance right for you.

Other ways of preparing for the PIRT

Further practice tests which are relevant to the PIRT are available in other books in this series. If you are interested in developing further your verbal usage skills (PIR1) and verbal logical reasoning skills (PIR4), we recommend that you use *How to Pass Verbal Reasoning Tests* (Tolley and Thomas). In addition to using the practice test, we suggest that you make use of the guidance offered in Chapter 2 of that book on the other points which you can do to improve your verbal usage and reasoning skills. Similarly, if your aim is to improve your numerical reasoning skills (PIR 3) we advise you to consult *How to Pass Numeracy Tests* (Tolley and Thomas). Once again, in addition to examples of different types of numeracy tests on which you can practice, suggestions are provided in Chapter 2 of *How to Pass Numeracy Tests* for things you can do to develop your competence in numerical reasoning. Further examples of clerical checking skills (PIR2) practice tests can be found in *How to Pass Selection Tests* (Bryon and Modha) and *How to Pass the Civil Service Qualifying Tests* (Bryon). Finally, do not overlook the guidance we have given in Chapter 8 on ways in which you can develop your observation skills (PIR5).

Chapter 4

PIR1 Verbal Usage Test

Introduction

In this test you will find sentences in which two gaps have been left. Your task is to decide what those missing words are. Below each sentence you will find four pairs of words, with a letter (A, B, C and D) above each pair. You have to work out which one of the pair of words fits into the spaces correctly. Sometimes it is a question of the spelling of the words or their meaning. On other occasions it is a matter of the correct use of grammar. In some of the items the right answer will be 'None of these', in which case you would record your decision by writing the letter E in the answer space provided. Working through the two examples given below should help you to understand what you have to do.

Example 1

Three police officers _____ present at the _____

A	B	C	D
was	was	were	were
enquirey	enquiry	enquiry	enquirey

E   None of these | Answer = C |

In this example the subject – that is, the 'Three police officers' – is third person plural. The correct form of the verb, therefore, is 'were' not 'was'. Had the sentence read 'The police officer' – that is, had the subject been singular not plural – the first missing word would have been 'was'. The second missing word is the one which is spelt correctly – that is, 'enquiry' not 'enquirey'. Now take a look at the second example.

Example 2

A witness was _____ talking to the _____.

A	B	C	D
scene	seen	scene	scene
suspect	susspect	susspect	suspect

E   None of these

> Answer = E

In this example with the first missing word it is not just a simple case of getting the correct spelling. The right answer is 'seen' which is part of the verb in the sentence. The word 'scene' is not only spelt differently but, because it is an object, it is a noun. The second word is 'suspect' (not 'susspect') because it is the one which is spelt correctly.

Three practice tests of this type are given below. Each test consists of 20 questions for which you should allow yourself 10 minutes per test – that is, half a minute per question. However, if you wish to put some pressure on yourself, try to do Test 3 in 8 minutes. Work as quickly and as accurately as you can. If you are not sure of an answer, mark your best choice, but avoid wild guessing. If you want to change an answer, rub it out completely and then write your new answer in the space provided. Give yourself one mark for each correct answer and make a note of scores to see if you are making any progress from one test to another. Remember to work carefully through any answers which you get wrong or fail to complete in the time allowed. In this subtest in the real PIRT, you will be allowed 12 minutes to answer 30 questions.

If you want to do some extra preparation for this particular sub test of the PIRT, you will find additional examples in Chapter 4 (Missing Words Tests) of *How to Pass Verbal Reasoning Tests* (Tolley and Thomas).

PIR1 Verbal usage tests

Test 1

1.   The _____ was in _____.

A	B	C	D
jury	jurey	jury	jurey
atendance	attendance	attendance	atendence

E   None of these   Answer =

2.   We went to _____ house to get the _____ details.

A	B	C	D
there	their	thier	there
relavent	relevant	relevant	relavant

E   None of these   Answer =

3.   The _____ said that the charge was _____.

A	B	C	D
accused	accused	acused	accoused
unfare	unfair	unfair	unfare

E   None of these   Answer =

4.   An accident_____ as they _____walking down the street.

A	B	C	D
occured	ocurred	ocurred	occurred
was	were	was	were

E   None of these   Answer =

5.   The offender was fined _____ pounds in _____.

A	B	C	D
fourty	fourty	forty	forty
February	Februry	February	Febuary

E   None of these   Answer =

6.   It _____ long until an _____ started.

A	B	C	D
wasn't	wasnt	was'nt	was'nt
argument	arguement	arguement	argument

E   None of these

Answer =

7.   The _____ was _____.

A	B	C	D
weather	whether	weather	whether
dissapointing	disappointing	disappointing	dissappointing

E   None of these

Answer =

8.   She was _____ upset about her _____ sentence.

A	B	C	D
extremley	extremeley	extremely	extremely
father's	fathers'	fathers	father's

E   None of these

Answer =

9.   She read her _____ rights and left _____.

A	B	C	D
statutory	statuary	statuory	statutary
imediately	immediately	immediatley	imediately

E   None of these

Answer =

10.   They had not done _____ enough to get_____.

A	B	C	D
good	well	good	well
promotion	promotion	premotion	premotion

E   None of these

Answer =

11.   The _____ was highly _____ to the recruits.

A	B	C	D
coarse	coarse	course	course
recommended	reccomended	recommended	recomeded

E   None of these

Answer =

12.   He was _____ on the _____ of March.

A	B	C	D
arrested	arested	aressted	arested
eighth	eigth	eigth	eighth

E   None of these | Answer = |

13.   The judge _____ the case very _____.

A	B	C	D
reviewed	reveiwed	reviewed	reveiwed
justly	just	just	justly

E   None of these | Answer = |

14.   _____ do you write to for the _____ information?

A	B	C	D
who	whom	whom	who
appropriate	apropriate	appropriate	apropriate

E   None of these | Answer = |

15.   The officer's _____ was _____.

A	B	C	D
absance	absence	absance	absence
unnecessary	unecessary	unnecesary	unnecessary

E   None of these | Answer = |

16.   The _____ accompanied the policeman and _____.

A	B	C	D
guard	gaurd	guard	gaurd
me	I	I	me

E   None of these | Answer = |

17.   The _____ showed a _____ rise in acts of crime.

A	B	C	D
annalysis	analysis	analisys	analysis
noticable	noticeable	noticible	noticable

E   None of these | Answer = |

18. He was _____ confused to write his _____.

A	B	C	D
to	two	too	too
address	addres	address	adress

E None of these

Answer = [ ]

19. Neither the man _____ the woman could _____ the statement.

A	B	C	D
or	or	nor	nor
corroborate	corobberate	coroborrate	corroborate

E None of these

Answer = [ ]

20. She _____ all the _____.

A	B	C	D
new	knew	knew	new
procedures	proceedures	procedures	proccedures

E None of these

Answer = [ ]

Test 2

1. The officer will attend at a _____ time on _____.

A	B	C	D
definite	definate	definate	definite
Wednesday	Wednesday	Wedensday	Wedensday

E None of these

Answer = [ ]

2. They _____ about it _____.

A	B	C	D
herd	heard	heard	herd
acidentley	accidentally	accidently	accidental

E None of these

Answer = [ ]

3. The lack of _____ was an _____.

A	B	C	D
planing	planning	planing	planning
embarassment	embarrasment	embarasment	embarrassment

E None of these

Answer = [ ]

4.   The event had lasted a _____ _____.

A	B	C	D
hole	hole	whole	whole
week	weak	week	weak

E   None of these

Answer =

5.   It was the _____ to book _____ well in advance.

A	B	C	D
practice	practise	practise	practice
acomodation	acomodation	acommodation	accommodation

E   None of these

Answer =

6.   He was _____ sorry about the _____ burglary.

A	B	C	D
truly	truley	truely	truly
agravated	aggravated	agrravated	aggravated

E   None of these

Answer =

7.   He _____that the bomb crater was 10 _____ wide.

A	B	C	D
believed	beleived	believed	beleived
metre	meters	metres	meter

E   None of these

Answer =

8.   The _____ voice had a note of _____.

A	B	C	D
soliciter's	solicitors'	solicitor's	soliciter's
anxierty	anxiety	anxiety	anxietty

E   None of these

Answer =

9.   The _____ _____ the data.

A	B	C	D
secerteries	secrataries	secritaries	secretaries
proccessed	processed	prossesed	processed

E   None of these

Answer =

10.   The women were _____ from the _____.

A	B	C	D
helpful	helpfull	helpfull	helpful
begining	begining	beginning	beggining

E   None of these

Answer =

11.   We know that _____ a great _____.

A	B	C	D
its'	it's	its	it's
priveledge	privilege	privilidge	privelage

E   None of these

Answer =

12.   He _____ that he would not_____ any evidence.

A	B	C	D
garunteed	guarranteed	guaranteed	gauranteed
withold	witholed	withhold	withold

E   None of these

Answer =

13.   The _____ had _____ shelter across the river.

A	B	C	D
fugitive	fugative	fugertive	fugitive
sort	saught	sought	sought

E   None of these

Answer =

14.   The _____ estate was very _____.

A	B	C	D
counsel	council	counsil	council
quite	quiet	quiet	quite

E   None of these

Answer =

15.   _____ it will be changed in the _____ year.

A	B	C	D
certainly	certainely	certinley	certenley
coming	comming	coming	comeing

E   None of these

Answer =

16.   He was afraid of _____ his _____.

A	B	C	D
loosing	lossing	loseing	losing
livelihood	livelyhood	livlihood	livelihood

E   None of these

Answer =

17.   The woman was _____to _____her promise.

A	B	C	D
desparate	desperate	desprate	desperate
fulfil	fulfill	fulfill	fulfil

E   None of these

Answer =

18.   The heavy fine was a _____ _____.

A	B	C	D
valuble	valuable	valuble	valueble
deterrent	deterrent	deterant	detterant

E   None of these

Answer =

19.   They think that the _____ _____ are unsatisfactory

A	B	C	D
currant	current	current	currant
criteria	criterion	criteria	criterion

E   None of these

Answer =

20.   The officer _____ the instructions from the _____.

A	B	C	D
received	recieved	recieved	received
sergeant	sargeant	sargent	sargant

E   None of these

Answer =

Test 3

1.   A _____ was elected to deal with cases of _____.

A	B	C	D
commitee	committee	committee	committee
harrassment	harrassment	harassment	harasment

E   None of these   Answer =

2.   The suspects were _____ _____.

A	B	C	D
interogated	interoggated	interrogated	interrogated
separate	seperately	seperate	separately

E   None of these   Answer =

3.   The _____ handed everyone a _____.

A	B	C	D
phsycologist	psychologist	psycologist	psycholigist
questionairre	questionnaire	questionair	questionaire

E   None of these   Answer =

4.   She _____ the thief as he was _____ out of the shop.

A	B	C	D
court	caught	caugth	caught
running	runing	running	runnin

E   None of these   Answer = E

5.   It was very easy to _____ the _____.

A	B	C	D
appreciate	apreceate	appreciate	apreciate
difficulty	dificculty	dificulty	difficulty

E   None of these   Answer =

6.   Her _____ still _____ said anything to her.

A	B	C	D
collagues	coleagues	colleages	colleagues
has'nt	hasn't	have'nt	haven't

E   None of these   Answer =

7. His _____ was given promotion and was _____.

A	B	C	D
predecesor	predecessor	predecceser	preddecesor
transfered	transferred	transferred	transfered

E   None of these   Answer =

8. He had_____ the speed limit and had to give a._____.

A	B	C	D
exceeded	exceded	exceeded	exceded
specimen	specimen	speciman	speciman

E   None of these   Answer =

9. It was _____ that the _____ had been granted.

A	B	C	D
suprising	serprising	surprising	supprising
license	license	licence	licence

E   None of these   Answer =

10. The _____ of high standards was _____ important.

A	B	C	D
maintainance	maintnance	maintenence	maintenance
undoutedly	undoutidly	undoubtedly	undoubtedly

E   None of these   Answer =

11. The _____ _____ watched the house for them.

A	B	C	D
niegbours	neighbours	nieghbours	niebhours
usauly	usually	usually	usualy

E   None of these   Answer =

12. The _____ was paid for by an _____ plan.

A	B	C	D
eqiupement	equipement	equipment	equippment
installment	installment	instalment	instalment

E   None of these   Answer =

13.　It was clear that they must _____ been very _____.

A	B	C	D
of	have	have	of
professionel	professional	proffesional	professional

E　None of these

Answer = (

14.　An _____ _____ had been invited to the enquiry.

A	B	C	D
independent	independant	independent	indapendant
observer	observor	observor	observer

E　None of these

Answer =

15.　The officer _____ that the _____ had not arrived.

A	B	C	D
regretted	regreted	reggreted	regretted
corespondence	correspondence	coresspondance	correspondence

E　None of these

Answer =

16.　The results of the examination _____ _____.

A	B	C	D
were	was	were	was
disasterous	dissastrous	disastrous	desastrous

E　None of these

Answer = (

17.　He had _____ to understand the reason for the _____.

A	B	C	D
begun	begun	began	began
critisism	criticism	critiscism	critisism

E　None of these

Answer =

18.　Each of the policemen _____ _____ had time to rest.

A	B	C	D
has	have	has	have
scarcely	scarcley	scaresly	scarsely

E　None of these

Answer =

19. She ＿＿ to the ＿＿ of the previous meeting.

A	B	C	D
refered	reffered	refered	referred
minites	minites	minnets	minutes

E None of these   Answer =

20. The judge said 'The ＿＿ of the error is ＿＿'.

A	B	C	D
repitition	repetition	repeatition	repatition
regretable	regrettable	regrettable	regretable

E None of these   Answer =

Answers to verbal usage tests

Test 1 (page 35)		**Test 2** (page 38)		**Test 3** (page 42)	
1.	C	1.	A	1.	C
2.	B	2.	B	2.	D
3.	B	3.	D	3.	B
4.	D	4.	C	4.	E
5.	C	5.	D	5.	A
6.	A	6.	D	6.	D
7.	C	7.	C	7.	B
8.	D	8.	C	8.	A
9.	E	9.	D	9.	C
10.	B	10.	E	10.	D
11.	C	11.	B	11.	B
12.	A	12.	C	12.	C
13.	A	13.	D	13.	B
14.	C	14.	B	14.	A
15.	D	15.	A	15.	D
16.	A	16.	D	16.	C
17.	B	17.	D	17.	B
18.	C	18.	B	18.	A
19.	D	19.	C	19.	D
20.	C	20.	A	20.	B

Chapter 5

PIR2 Checking Test

Introduction

In this test you have to check that the information in a type-written list (given on the left-hand page) has been transcribed correctly to a computer screen (shown on the right-hand page). The information is about goods – for example, bicycles, cars and television sets – which have been reported as stolen to the police over a four month period. The layout of the information on the computer screen is different from that used for the type-written list. Your task is to compare the two lists with a view to finding any errors – that is, differences or omissions. Your answers have to be recorded in the appropriate spaces on the answer sheet as follows:

Fill in space A if there are errors in column 1 of the computer screen.

Fill in space B if there are errors in column 2 of the computer screen.

Fill in space C if there are errors in column 3 of the computer screen.

Fill in space D if there are errors in column 4 of the computer screen.

Only fill in space E if there are no errors on that particular line.

Now take a look at the examples given below. Mark your answers in the spaces given below the computer screen.

| 1 | Name: Woods | (Mr) Mrs Miss Ms | Date: 8 October |
| | Car make & model: | Green Ford Mondeo | Engine no: HZ41325 |

2	Name: Lines	Mr Mrs Miss (Ms)	Date: 11 October	
	Car make & model:	Red VW Vento	Engine no: 20HG72198	

| A | B | C | D | E |

3	Name: Page	Mr (Mrs) Miss Ms	Date: 4 October	
	Car make & model:	Blue Mercedes	Engine no: FG51361	

4	Name: Alton	(Mr) Mrs Miss Ms	Date: 20 October	
	Car make & model:	Silver Honda Civic	Engine no: 1300G854	

	Column 1 Date: reported (day/month)	Column 2 Description	Column 3 Engine no	Column 4 Owner's name & title	
1.	8/10	Green Ford Mondeo	HZ41235	Wood	Mr
2.	10/11	Red VW Vento	20HG72198	Lines	Ms
3.	4/10	Blue Mercedes	FG51361	Page	Mrs
4.	20/10	Grey Honda Civic	1300G854	Allton	Mr

1.	☐	☐	☐	☐	☐
2.	☐	☐	☐	☐	☐
3.	☐	☐	☐	☐	☐
4.	☐	☐	☐	☐	☐

Four practice tests of this type are given below. Tests 1, 2 and 3 each consist of 20 questions. Allow yourself 6 minutes per test. Test 4 contains 30 questions which you should try to answer in 8 minutes. Work as quickly and as accurately as you can. If you are not sure of an answer, mark your best choice, but as usual the advice is to avoid wild guessing. If you want to change an answer, rub it out completely and then write your new answer in the box provided. Give yourself one mark for each correct answer and make a note of the scores to see if you are improving from one test to another. In this sub test in the real PIRT, you will be allowed 8 minutes to answer 30 questions.

Answers

1. = C and D   2. = A   3. = E   4. = B and D

Test 1

1. Name: Allerton   Mr Mrs Miss (Ms)   Date: 8 October
   Car make & model: Red Mercedes   Engine no: 316297

2. Name: Coghlan   Mr (Mrs) Miss Ms   Date: 14 January
   Car make & model: Ford Fiesta L   Engine no: 293467

3. Name: Faulds   Mr Mrs (Miss) Ms   Date: 4 February
   Car make & model: Leyland Mini Mayfair   Engine no: 638149

4. Name: Huggett   (Mr) Mrs Miss Ms   Date: 11 July
   Car make & model: Blue Renault Estate   Engine no: 884281

5. Name: Macisaac   (Mr) Mrs Miss Ms   Date: 12 June
   Car make & model: Green Daihatsu Fourtrak   Engine no: 211334

6. Name: Oakship   Mr Mrs Miss (Ms)   Date: 2 March
   Car make & model: Yellow Toyota Estate   Engine no: 455681

7. Name: Nouillan   Mr Mrs (Miss) Ms   Date: 2 September
   Car make & model: Black Porsche   Engine no: 114229

	Column 1 Date reported day/month	Column 2 Description	Column 3 Engine no	Column 4 Owner's name & title	
1.	8/10	Red Mercedes	312697	Allerton	Ms
2.	14/2	Ford Fiesta	293467	Coghlan	Mrs
3.	4/2	Leyland Mini Mayfair	638149	Faulds	Miss
4.	11/6	Blue Renault Estate	884281	Huggett	Mr
5.	12/6	Green Daihatsu Fourtrak	213314	Macisac	Ms
6.	3/2	Yellow Toyota Estate	455681	Oakship	Mr
7.	2/9	Black Porshe	1114229	Nouillan	Miss

1 A ☐	B ☐	C ☐	D ☐	E ☐
2. A ☐	B ☐	C ☐	D ☐	E ☐
3. A ☐	B ☐	C ☐	D ☐	E ☐
4. A ☐	B ☐	C ☐	D ☐	E ☐
5. A ☐	B ☐	C ☐	D ☐	E ☐
6. A ☐	B ☐	C ☐	D ☐	E ☐
7. A ☐	B ☐	C ☐	D ☐	E ☐

8. Name: Reid   Mr (Mrs) Miss Ms   Date: 6 April
   Car make & model: Orange Ford Escort   Engine no: 248793

9. Name: Patel   (Mr) Mrs Miss Ms   Date: 9 November
   Car make & model: White Volvo Estate   Engine no: 448861

10. Name: Verben   Mr Mrs (Miss) Ms   Date: 26 May
    Car make & model: Green Volkswagen   Engine no: 219776
                       Convertible

11. Name: Freedic   Mr Mrs (Miss) Ms   Date: 8 February
    Car make & model: Daihatsu 4WD   Engine no: 29342

12. Name: Jessiman   Mr Mrs Miss (Ms)   Date: 14 March
    Car make & model: Yellow Golf Turbo   Engine no: 97700

13. Name: Muir   Mr (Mrs) Miss Ms   Date: 27 August
    Car make & model: Cream Ford Fiesta   Engine no: 83212

14. Name: Rustoll   (Mr) Mrs Miss Ms   Date: 18 April
    Car make & model: Red Two Door Skoda   Engine no: 34756

	Column 1 Date reported day/month	Column 2 Description	Column 3 Engine no	Column 4 Owner's name & title	
8.	6/4	Orange Ford Escort	248793	Reid	Mrs
9.	9/9	White Volvo Estate	4488611	Patel	Mr
10.	26/5	Green Volksloagan Convertible	29776	Verben	Miss
11.	8/2	Dihatsui 4WD	29342	Freedie	Miss
12.	14/3	Yellow Golf Turbo	977000	Jessiman	Mr
13.	27/7	Green Ford Fiesta	83213	Muir	Mrs
14.	18/5	Red Two Door Scoda	34756	Rustoll	Mr

8. A ☐ B ☐ C ☐ D ☐ E ☑

9. A ☐ B ☐ C ☐ D ☐ E ☐

10. A ☐ B ☐ C ☐ D ☐ E ☐

11. A ☐ B ☐ C ☐ D ☑ E ☐

12. A ☐ B ☐ C ☑ D ☐ E ☐

13. A ☐ B ☐ C ☐ D ☐ E ☐

14. A ☐ B ☐ C ☐ D ☐ E ☐

15. Name: Waddell   Mr Mrs (Miss) Ms   Date: 27 May
    Car make & model: Peugot Convertible   Engine no: 20197

16. Name: Devanha   (Mr) Mrs Miss Ms   Date: 23 September
    Car make & model: Beige Saab Turbo   Engine no: 00362

17. Name: Frippak   Mr Mrs (Miss) Ms   Date: 21 October
    Car make & model: Long Wheel Base   Engine no: 84015
                          Landrover

18. Name: Wacht   Mr Mrs Miss (Ms)   Date: 10 July
    Car make & model: Orange Lada Estate   Engine no: 77313

19. Name: Denoon   Mr (Mrs) Miss Ms   Date: 16 March
    Car make & model: Mercedes Convertible Engine no: 22368

20. Name: Claughan   (Mr) Mrs Miss Ms   Date: 6 December
    Car make & model: Green Ford Sierra   Engine no: 62934

	Column 1 Date reported day/month	Column 2 Description	Column 3 Engine no	Column 4 Owner's name & title
15.	27/5	Puegot Convertible	20917	Waddell Miss
16.	23/9	Beige Saab Turbo	00362	Devanha Mr
17.	21/10	Long Wheel Based Landrover	84105	Frippack Ms
18.	7/10	Orange Lada Estate	777131	Wacht Mr
19.	16/3	Mercedes Convertible	22368	Denoon Mrs
20.	12/6	Green Ford Siera	62934	Claughan Mr

15. A ☐   B ☐   C ☐   D ☐   E ☐
16. A ☐   B ☐   C ☐   D ☐   E ☑
17. A ☐   B ☑   C ☑   D ☑   E ☐
18. A ☑   B ☐   C ☐   D ☐   E ☐
19. A ☐   B ☐   C ☐   D ☐   E ☐
20. A ☐   B ☐   C ☐   D ☐   E ☐

Test 2

1. Name: Catto Mr (Mrs) Miss Ms Date: 11 January
   Television make: Panasonic XR Serial no: 6293HZ

2. Name: Dudgeon Mr Mrs Miss (Ms) Date: 19 August
   Television make: Sony XRS Serial no: 1141DT

3. Name: Foswell Mr Mrs (Miss) Ms Date: 20 December
   Television make: Philips XXT Serial no: 2190ZR

4. Name: Gourlay (Mr) Mrs Miss Ms Date: 23 March
   Television make: Matsui SS Serial no: 5543GJ

5. Name: Healey Mr (Mrs) Miss Ms Date: 31 October
   Television make: Ferguson Deluxe Serial no: 3008TZ

6. Name: Laing Mr Mrs Miss (Ms) Date: 25 May
   Television make: Mitsubishi TRS Serial no: 2981JL

7. Name: Lorimer Mr Mrs (Miss) Ms Date: 14 June
   Television make: JVC XTR Serial no: 8132KL

	Column 1 Date reported day/month	Column 2 Description	Column 3 Engine no	Column 4 Owner's name & title	
1.	11/11	Panasonic XX	6293HZ	Catto	Mr
2.	19/9	Sony XRS	11141DT	Dudgen	Ms
3.	20/12	Phillips XXT	2190ZR	Foswell	Miss
4.	23/3	Matsuii SS	543GJ	Gourlay	Mr
5.	31/10	Ferguson Deluxe	3008TZ	Healey	Mrs
6.	25/6	Mitsuibishi TRS	2981JL	Laing	Ms
7.	6/14	JVC TXR	81312KL	Lorimer	Miss

1. A ☐   B ☐   C ☐   D ☐   E ☐
2. A ☐   B ☐   C ☐   D ☐   E ☐
3. A ☐   B ☐   C ☐   D ☐   E ☐
4. A ☐   B ☐   C ☐   D ☐   E ☐
5. A ☐   B ☐   C ☐   D ☐   E ☐
6. A ☐   B ☐   C ☐   D ☐   E ☐
7. A ☐   B ☐   C ☐   D ☐   E ☐

8. Name: MacFarn   Mr Mrs Miss (Ms)   Date: 29 March
    Television make: ITT Deluxe   Serial no: 6686ZT

9. Name: Mairer   Mr (Mrs) Miss Ms   Date: 13 February
    Television make: Matsui Deluxe   Serial no: 0010TS

10. Name: Protze   (Mr) Mrs Miss Ms   Date: 23 July
    Television make: Mitsubishi Mini XX   Serial no: 7734KN

11. Name: Knoeffe   Mr Mrs Miss (Ms)   Date: 7 June
    Television make: Portable Saisho L   Serial no: JZ0130

12. Name: Cabrelli   Mr Mrs (Miss) Ms   Date: 13 February
    Television make: Philips Black and White Serial no: TF1921

13. Name: Farguhar   Mr (Mrs) Miss Ms   Date: 25 October
    Television make: Sanyo Colour XXR   Serial no: JF1880

14. Name: Leggat   (Mr) Mrs Miss Ms   Date: 31 January
    Television make: Mitsubishi Portable   Serial no: QR1223

	Column 1 Date reported day/month	Column 2 Description	Column 3 Engine no	Column 4 Owner's name & title	
8.	29/3	ITT Deluxe	6686ZT	MacFarn	Ms
9.	13/2	Matsui Delux	00110TS	Marer	Mrs
10.	23/6	Mitsubishi Mini XX	7743KN	Prozte	Mr
11.	6/7	Portable Sashio L	JZ1030	Knoeffe	Ms
12.	13/2	Philips Black and White	TF1921	Cabrelli	Miss
13.	25/10	Sanjo Colour XXR	JF8180	Farguha	Mrs
14.	30/1	Mitsuibishi Portable	QR11223	Leggat	Mr

	A	B	C	D	E
8.	☐	☐	☐	☐	☑
9.	☐	☐	☐	☐	☐
10.	☐	☐	☐	☐	☐
11.	☐	☐	☐	☐	☐
12.	☐	☐	☐	☐	☐
13.	☐	☐	☐	☐	☐
14.	☑	☐	☐	☐	☐

15. Name: McKenzies   Mr Mrs (Miss) Ms   Date: 17 March
    Television make: Ferguson Stereo TV   Serial no: NT0157

16. Name: Sheedin   Mr Mrs Miss (Ms)   Date: 21 November
    Television make: Aiwa Portable L5   Serial no: VB2215

17. Name: Zaccarine   Mr (Mrs) Miss Ms   Date: 19 August
    Television make: Matsui Black and White Serial no: TU0019

18. Name: Younie   Mr Mrs Miss (Ms)   Date: 1 May
    Television make: Philips Colour XSR   Serial no: YH6721

19. Name: Byers   (Mr) Mrs Miss Ms   Date: 22 December
    Television make: JVC Colour Portable   Serial no: CQ4377

20. Name: Burrell   Mr Mrs (Miss) Ms   Date: 29 April
    Television make: Technic Black and White Serial no: SY6537

	Column 1 Date reported day/month	Column 2 Description	Column 3 Engine no	Column 4 Owner's name & title	
15.	17/3	Ferguson Stereo TV	NT01577	McKensie	Ms
16.	21/12	Aiwa Portable L5	VP22125	Sheeden	Ms
17.	19/8	Matsui Black and White	TU0019	Zaccarine	Mrs
18.	5/1	Phillips Colour Portable	YH6721	Youni	Mr
19.	22/12	JCV Colour Portable	CQ4377	Byiers	Ms
20.	29/6	Technic Black and White	SY65137	Burrell	Miss

15. A ☐   B ☐   C ☐   D ☐   E ☐

16. A ☑   B ☐   C ☐   D ☐   E ☐

17. A ☐   B ☐   C ☐   D ☐   E ☑

18. A ☐   B ☑   C ☐   D ☐   E ☐

19. A ☐   B ☐   C ☐   D ☐   E ☐

20. A ☐   B ☐   C ☐   D ☐   E ☐

Test 3

---

1. Name: Cuthill   Mr (Mrs) Miss Ms   Date: 18 March
    Bicycle model: Raleigh Sprinter   Serial no: TP001451

---

2. Name: Fyvie   Mr Mrs Miss (Ms)   Date: 21 April
    Bicycle model: Off-Road Mountain Bike   Serial no: ZR441392

---

3. Name: Graham   (Mr) Mrs Miss Ms   Date: 11 May
    Bicycle model: Dawes All Terrain Bike   Serial no: BT391461

---

4. Name: Kincorth   Mr Mrs (Miss) Ms   Date: 23 July
    Bicycle model: Peugot 10 Gear Racer   Serial no: TD413210

---

5. Name: Maines   Mr Mrs (Miss) Ms   Date: 14 January
    Bicycle model: Saracen Tourer   Serial no: XN655771

---

6. Name: Tytler   (Mr) Mrs Miss Ms   Date: 27 September
    Bicycle model: Claud Butler Scrambler   Serial no: SP437991

---

7. Name: Robertson Mr Mrs Miss (Ms)   Date: 13 December
    Bicycle model: Apollo 18 Gear Tourer   Serial no: RC566190

	Column 1 Date reported day/month	Column 2 Description	Column 3 Engine no	Column 4 Owner's name & title	
1.	18/5	Releigh Sprinter	TP001451	Cutill	Mrs
2.	21/4	Off-Road Mountain Bike	Z441392	Fyvie	Ms
3.	11/5	Dawes All Terain Bike	BR391461	Graham	Mr
4.	23/6	Peugot 18 Gear Racer	TD413210	Kincoth	Miss
5.	1/14	Saracen Tourer	NX655577	Maines	Miss
6.	27/9	Claud Butler Scrambler	SP437991	Tyler	Ms
7.	12/13	Appolo 18 Gear Tourer	RC556190	Robertson	Ms

1. A ☐ B ☐ C ☐ D ☐ E ☐
2. A ☐ B ☐ C ☐ D ☐ E ☐
3. A ☐ B ☐ C ☐ D ☐ E ☐
4. A ☐ B ☐ C ☐ D ☐ E ☐
5. A ☐ B ☐ C ☐ D ☐ E ☐
6. A ☐ B ☐ C ☐ D ☐ E ☐
7. A ☐ B ☐ C ☐ D ☐ E ☐

8. Name: Newten   Mr (Mrs) Miss Ms   Date: 12 May
    Bicycle model: Holdsworth Classic   Serial no: NH431199

9. Name: Biscous   (Mr) Mrs Miss Ms   Date: 3 January
    Bicycle model: Dawes All Terrain Scrambler   Serial no: VW267589

10. Name: Patel   Mr Mrs Miss (Ms)   Date: 4 June
    Bicycle model: Nigel Dean Super Tourer   Serial no: XQ198810

11. Name: Gough   Mr Mrs (Miss) Ms   Date: 10 October
    Bicycle model: Holdsworth 5 Gear Shopper   Serial no: ZW419660

12. Name: Ritchie   Mr (Mrs) Miss Ms   Date: 17 February
    Bicycle model: Peugot 20 Gear Racer   Serial no: BV117558

13. Name: Pittard   Mr Mrs Miss (Ms)   Date: 24 June
    Bicycle model: Diamond Back ATB   Serial no: KP001567

14. Name: Nvocson   (Mr) Mrs Miss Ms   Date: 12 May
    Bicycle model: Saracen Tandem Tourer   Serial no: ZP397761

	Column 1 Date reported day/month	Column 2 Description	Column 3 Engine no	Column 4 Owner's name & title	
8.	12/5	Holdsworth Classic	NH431199	Newten	Mrs
9.	3/1	Dawes All Terrain Scrambler	VW267589	Biscous	Mr
10.	4/6	Nigel Daen Super Tours	XQ1988810	Patel	Mr
11.	10/10	Holdsworth 5 Gear Shopper	ZW491660	Cough	Miss
12.	17/3	Peugot 20 Gear Racer	BV171558	Ritchie	Mrs
13.	24/7	Diamond Back ABT	KP001567	Pittrad	Ms
14.	12/5Saracen Tandem Tourer		ZP397761	Nvocson	Mr

8. A ☐   B ☐   C ☐   D ☐   E ☐

9. A ☐   B ☐   C ☐   D ☐   E ☐

10. A ☐   B ☐   C ☐   D ☐   E ☐

11. A ☐   B ☐   C ☐   D ☐   E ☐

12. A ☐   B ☐   C ☐   D ☐   E ☐

13. A ☐   B ☐   C ☐   D ☐   E ☐

14. A ☐   B ☐   C ☐   D ☐   E ☐

15. Name: McIrvine (Mr) Mrs Miss Ms   Date: 27 November
    Bicycle model: Raleigh Tots Scooter   Serial no: RS455611

16. Name: Linklater   Mr Mrs (Miss) Ms   Date: 2 March
    Bicycle model: Nigel Dean 12 Gear   Serial no: GF019865
                  Tourer

17. Name: Jeromson   Mr (Mrs) Miss Ms   Date: 4 August
    Bicycle model: Holdsworth Tricycle   Serial no: QR321900

18. Name: Goudlie   Mr Mrs Miss (Ms)   Date: 17 July
    Bicycle model: Off-Road 10 Gear   Serial no: MN174331
                  Scrambler

19. Name: Singh   Mr Mrs Miss (Ms)   Date: 23 June
    Bicycle model: Apollo 3 Speed Fold   Serial no: YW981181
                  Away

20. Name: Benoites   Mr (Mrs) Miss Ms   Date: 18 September
    Bicycle model: Claud Butler Racer   Serial no: KC217151

	Column 1 Date reported day/month	Column 2 Description	Column 3 Engine no	Column 4 Owner's name & title
15.	27/9	Raleigh Tot Scooter	RS445611	McIrvine Mr
16.	2/3	Nigel Dean 18 Gear Tourer	GF091866	Linlater Miss
17.	4/4	Holdsworth Tricycle	QR312900	Jeromsen Ms
18.	17/7	Off-Road 10 Gar Scrambler	MN174331	Goudie Mr
19.	23/6	Apollo 3 Speed Fold Away	YW981181	Singh Ms
20.	18/7	Cluad Buter Racer	KC271515	Benoites Mrs

15. A ☐ B ☐ C ☐ D ☐ E ☐
16. A ☐ B ☐ C ☐ D ☐ E ☐
17. A ☐ B ☐ C ☐ D ☐ E ☐
18. A ☐ B ☐ C ☐ D ☐ E ☐
19. A ☐ B ☐ C ☐ D ☐ E ☐
20. A ☐ B ☐ C ☐ D ☐ E ☐

Test 4

1. Name: Bichan   Mr Mrs Miss (Ms)   Date: 7 March
   Car make & model: Black Ferrari   Engine no: 493321X

2. Name: Heinemeier   Mr (Mrs) Miss Ms   Date: 12 April
   Car make & model: Blue Volvo Estate   Engine no: 329781J

3. Name: McColl   Mr Mrs Miss (Ms)   Date: 19 December
   Car make & model: Yellow Citroen 2CV   Engine no: 457621T

4. Name: O'Reary   (Mr) Mrs Miss Ms   Date: 28 June
   Car make & model: Green Suzuki TX   Engine no: 331789F

5. Name: Stronacht   Mr Mrs (Miss) Ms   Date: 9 November
   Car make & model: 4 Door Ford Escort   Engine no: 201314X

6. Name: Voyzey   Mr Mrs Miss (Ms)   Date: 12 September
   Car make & model: Beige Fiat Uno   Engine no: 015575E

	Column 1 Date reported day/month	Column 2 Description	Column 3 Engine no	Column 4 Owner's name & title	
1.	5/7	Black Ferarri	493321X	Bichan	Ms
2.	12/5	Blue Volvo Estate	32981J	Hienemeier	Mrs
3.	19/12	Yellow Citreon 2CV	4576121T	McColl	Ms
4.	28/7	Green Suziuki TX	3131789F	O-Rearey	Ms
5.	9/9	4 Door Ford Escort	201314X	Stronach	Miss
6.	12/9	Beige Fiat Uno	015575E	Voyzey	Ms

1. A ☐   B ☐   C ☐   D ☐   E ☐
2. A ☐   B ☐   C ☐   D ☐   E ☐
3. A ☐   B ☐   C ☐   D ☐   E ☐
4. A ☐   B ☐   C ☐   D ☐   E ☐
5. A ☐   B ☐   C ☐   D ☐   E ☐
6. A ☐   B ☐   C ☐   D ☐   E ☐

7. Name: Wilsons   (Mr) Mrs Miss Ms   Date: 23 January
    Car make & model: Peugot 205   Engine no: 566217RT
                           Convertible

8. Name: Ravi   Mr (Mrs) Miss Ms   Date: 10 August
    Car make & model: Red Montego Estate   Engine no: 298817B

9. Name: Bennett   Mr Mrs (Miss) Ms   Date: 29 May
    Car make & model: White Vauxhall   Engine no: 332187P
                          Cavalier

10. Name: Sishnu   Mr Mrs Miss (Ms)   Date: 17 June
    Car make & model: Pink Bedford Van   Engine no: 134621N

11. Name: Alphonse   Mr (Mrs) Miss Ms   Date: 3 March
    Television make: Philips Black and   Serial no: 122321RT
                         White

12. Name: Belland   Mr Mrs Miss (Ms)   Date: 4 August
    Television make: ITT Colour XXR   Serial no: 297140PO

	Column 1 Date reported day/month	Column 2 Description	Column 3 Engine no	Column 4 Owner's name & title	
7.	23/1	Peugot 250 Convertible	556217RT	Wilson	Mr
8.	10/9	Red Monetego Estate	219887B	Ravi	Mrs
9.	29/4	White Vauxhall Cavalier	332187B	Benett	Miss
10.	17/6	Pink Bedford Van	134621N	Sishnu	Ms
11.	3/5	Phillips Black and White	123221RT	Alphonse	Mrs
12.	4/8	ITT Colour XXR	297140PO	Belland	Ms

7. A ☐   B ☐   C ☐   D ☐   E ☐

8. A ☐   B ☐   C ☐   D ☐   E ☐

9. A ☐   B ☐   C ☐   D ☐   E ☐

10. A ☐   B ☐   C ☐   D ☐   E ☐

11. A ☐   B ☐   C ☐   D ☐   E ☐

12. A ☐   B ☐   C ☐   D ☐   E ☐

13. Name: Chandler　(Mr) Mrs Miss Ms　　　Date: 21 December
    Television make:　Matsui Colour Stereo　　Serial no: 346571BT

14. Name: Davidson　Mr (Mrs) Miss Ms　　　Date: 9 February
    Television make:　Aiwa Sonic Super　　Serial no: 430109TF

15. Name: Govers　Mr Mrs (Miss) Ms　　　Date: 19 July
    Television make:　Mitsubishi Portable TSR　Serial no: 739122JL

16. Name: Revendra　Mr Mrs Miss (Ms)　　　Date: 8 October
    Television make:　Sony Visual Extra　　Serial no: 014795XR

17. Name: Kingsley　(Mr) Mrs Miss Ms　　　Date: 12 June
    Television make:　Sanyo Black and White　Serial no: 871433BS
    　　　　　　　　　TXR

18. Name: Polloque　Mr Mrs (Miss) Ms　　　Date: 24 January
    Television make:　Saisho Colour Monitor　Serial no: 441972MJ

	Column 1 Date reported day/month	Column 2 Description	Column 3 Engine no	Column 4 Owner's name & title
3.	21/12	Matsu Colour Stero	345671BT	Chandler Mr
4.	9/3	Awia Sonic Stereo	430109TF	Davison Mrs
5.	19/7	Mitsubishi Portable TSR	7391122JE	Govers Ms
6.	8/8	Sonya Visual XTRA	014759XR	Revendra Ms
7.	12/6	Sanyo Black and White TXR	871433BS	Kingsley Mr
8.	24/1	Sasho Colour Montor	449172NJ	Poloque Miss

13.   A ☐   B ☐   C ☐   D ☐   E ☐
14.   A ☐   B ☐   C ☐   D ☐   E ☐
15.   A ☐   B ☐   C ☐   D ☐   E ☐
16.   A ☐   B ☐   C ☐   D ☐   E ☐
17.   A ☐   B ☐   C ☐   D ☐   E ☐
18.   A ☐   B ☐   C ☐   D ☐   E ☐

19. Name: Scothson   Mr (Mrs) Miss Ms   Date: 26 May
    Television make: Technic Handset TXR   Serial no: 321578DK

20. Name: Urybank   Mr Mrs (Miss) Ms   Date: 1 April
    Television make: JVC Audio Colour SXR   Serial no: 411081DF

21. Name: Glennie   Mr Mrs Miss (Ms)   Date: 8 October
    Bicycle model: Apollo 21 inch Tandem   Serial no: VP001932

22. Name: Donegue   Mr (Mrs) Miss Ms   Date: 21 March
    Bicycle model: Diamond Back Racer   Serial no: QR313122

23. Name: Cooper   Mr Mrs (Miss) Ms   Date: 1 February
    Bicycle model: Raleigh 5 Gear Racer   Serial no: KL415651

24. Name: Chang   (Mr) Mrs Miss Ms   Date: 4 September
    Bicycle model: Off-Road ATB   Serial no: MB837431

	Column 1 Date reported day/month	Column 2 Description	Column 3 Engine no	Column 4 Owner's name & title	
19.	5/26	Tecnic Hand Set TTXR	321578DK	Scothson	Mrs
20.	1/1	JVC Audio Colour SXR	1411081DF	Urrybank	Miss
21.	8/8	Apollo 21 Inch Tandem	VF009132	Glenie	Ms
22.	21/3	Dimond Back Racer	QR312132	Donegue	Mrs
23.	1/2	Raleigh 5 Gear Racer	LK415651	Cooper	Ms
24.	4/9	Off-Road ATB	MB837431	Chang	Mr

19. A ☐   B ☐   C ☐   D ☐   E ☐

20. A ☐   B ☐   C ☐   D ☐   E ☐

21. A ☐   B ☐   C ☐   D ☐   E ☐

22. A ☐   B ☐   C ☐   D ☐   E ☐

23. A ☐   B ☐   C ☐   D ☐   E ☐

24. A ☐   B ☐   C ☐   D ☐   E ☐

25. Name: Breslin   Mr Mrs Miss (Ms)   Date: 19 November
    Bicycle model: Saracen Top Tourer   Serial no: CD249638

26. Name: Vantino   (Mr) Mrs Miss Ms   Date: 18 May
    Bicycle model: Peugot High Top Racer   Serial no: EF333151

27. Name: Leslie   Mr Mrs (Miss) Ms   Date: 25 July
    Bicycle model: Nigel Dean Tricycle   Serial no: GX249811

28. Name: Reaves   Mr (Mrs) Miss Ms   Date: 6 January
    Bicycle model: Giant Mountain Bike   Serial no: YT347756

29. Name: Paterson   Mr Mrs Miss (Ms)   Date: 14 August
    Bicycle model: Claud Butler Classic   Serial no: SR311009

30. Name: Satu   Mr (Mrs) Miss Ms   Date: 6 July
    Bicycle model: Peugot Cobra ATB   Serial no: AK432191

	Column 1 Date reported day/month	Column 2 Description	Column 3 Engine no	Column 4 Owner's name & title	
25.	19/9	Scaracen Top Tourer	CD249638	Breslin	Ms
26.	18/5	Puegot High Top Racer	EF333515	Vanitino	Mr
27.	25/6	Nigel Dean Tricycle	GX2491811	Leslie	Miss
28.	1/6	Gaint Mountain Bicycle	YT347756	Reavse	Mrs
29.	14/8	Claud Buttler Clasic	SR311009	Patterson	Ms
30.	6/7	Peugot Cobra ATB	AK432191	Satu	Mrs

25. A ☐ B ☐ C ☐ D ☐ E ☐
26. A ☐ B ☐ C ☐ D ☐ E ☐
27. A ☐ B ☐ C ☐ D ☐ E ☐
28. A ☐ B ☐ C ☐ D ☐ E ☐
29. A ☐ B ☐ C ☐ D ☐ E ☐
30. A ☐ B ☐ C ☐ D ☐ E ☐

Answers to checking tests

Test 1 (page 50)	**Test 2** (page 56)	**Test 3** (page 62)	**Test 4** (page 68)
1. C	1. A, B, D	1. A, B, D	1. A, B
2. A, B	2. A, C, D	2. C	2. A, C, D
3. E	3. B	3. B, C	3. B, C
4. A	4. B, C	4. A, B, D	4. A, B, C, D
5. C, D	5. E	5. A, C	5. A, D
6. A, D	6. A, B	6. D	6. E
7. B, C	7. A, B, C	7. A, B, C	7. B, C, D
8. D E	8. E	8. E	8. A, B, C
9. A, C	9. B, C, D	9. E	9. A, C, D
10. B, C	10. A, C, D	10. B, C, D	10. E
11. B, D	11. A, B, C	11. C, D	11. A, B, C
12. C, D	12. E	12. A, C	12. E
13. A, B, C	13. B, C, D	13. A, B, D	13. B, C
14. A, B	14. A, B, C	14. E	14. A, B, D
15. C	15. C, D	15. A, B, C	15. C, D
16. E	16. A, C, D	16. B, C, D	16 A, B, C
17. B, C, D	17. E	17. A, C, D	17. E
18. A, C, D	18. A, B, D	18. B, D	18. B, C, D
19. E	19. B, C, D	19. E	19. A, B
20. A, B	20. A, C	20. A, B, C	20. A, C, D
			21. A, C, D
			22. B, C
			23. C, D
			24. E
			25. A, B
			26. B, C, D
			27. A, C
			28. A, B, D
			29. B, D
			30. E

16/20   17/20   14/20

Chapter 6

PIR3 Numerical Reasoning Test

Introduction

In this test you are presented with a fairly simple and straight-forward number problem and required to select the correct answer from five possible answers. The number problems in this test are based on the four basic arithmetical rules:

- addition;
- subtraction;
- multiplication;
- division.

They also involve simple:

- fractions;
- decimals;
- averages;
- percentages.

You are required to apply these basic arithmetical operations in order to calculate:

- quantities of money;
- numbers of objects;
- speed;
- time;
- area.

Since you are not allowed to use a calculator in the PIRT, you should try to work without one whenever you can. This applies particularly when you are attempting the practice tests. It is a good idea, however, to use one at the end to check your answers.

The two examples given below should help you to get the idea before you start on the practice tests themselves.

Example 1

How much money would it cost to buy seven loaves of bread at 52p a loaf?

A	B	C	D	E
£3.44	£3.54	£3.64	£3.74	£3.84

Answer = ☐ C

Example 2

If I pay £4.56 for a tin of paint and 85p for a brush, how much will I have spent in total?

A	B	C	D	E
£5.31	£5.41	£5.51	£5.61	£5.71

Answer = ☐ B

Three practice tests of this type are given below. Each test consists of 20 questions, for which you should allow yourself 10 minutes per test. If you want to put some pressure on yourself, try to do Test 3 in 8 minutes. Work as quickly and as accurately as you can. Use a sheet of paper or a notepad for any rough work. If you are not sure of an answer, mark your best choice, but avoid wild guessing. If you want to change an answer, rub it out completely and then write your new answer in the space provided. Give yourself one mark for each correct answer and make a note of the scores to see if you are improving from one test to another. In the PIRT you will be allowed 12 minutes to answer 30 questions in this subtest.

If you want to do some extra preparation for this particular sub test of the PIRT, you will find additional examples in Chapter 4 of *How to Pass Numeracy Tests* (Tolley and Thomas).

Test 1

1. How much will five tins of soup cost at 55p a tin?

A	B	C	D	E
£2.25	£2.55	£2.60	£2.75	£2.95

   Answer = [D]

2. A person saves £35 in four weeks. At this rate how much will have been saved in one year?

A	B	C	D	E
£200	£250	£355	£420	£455

   Answer = [D]

3. What is the total cost of a journey when £1.65 is spent on bus-fares and an Underground ticket costs £2.50?

A	B	C	D	E
£3.15	£3.60	£3.95	£4.05	£4.15

   Answer = [ ]

4. What is the average number of people per car, when six cars carry thirty people?

A	B	C	D	E
4.5	5.0	5.5	6.0	6.5

   Answer = [ ]

5. If shopping items cost £12.64, how much money remains out of £20?

A	B	C	D	E
£6.36	£6.63	£7.36	£7.46	£7.63

   Answer = [C]

6. A car is travelling at 64 miles per hour. How many miles will it have travelled in 45 minutes?

A	B	C	D	E
40	44	46	48	50

   Answer = [ ]

7. Six magazines contain 120 pages each. How many pages are there in total?

A	B	C	D	E
620	720	760	780	820

Answer = ☐

8. A researcher interviews one household out of every eight in a village of 240 households. How many interviews take place?

A	B	C	D	E
12	24	30	32	36

Answer = ☐

9. If my weekly paper bill is £3.20 and the delivery charge is an extra 35p, how much do I have to pay over six weeks?

A	B	C	D	E
£19.20	£19.65	£20.20	£20.30	£21.30

Answer = ☐

10. Items costing £2.50, £3.10 and £4.40 are bought out of the petty cash which contains £30. What percentage of the cash is left?

A	B	C	D	E
30.33%	33.33%	60.50%	66.66%	77.77%

Answer = ☐

11. Number of foggy days

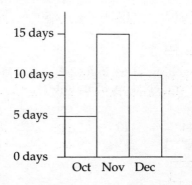

What is the average number of foggy days per month over this three month period?

A	B	C	D	E
5	7.5	10	15	17.5

Answer = ☐

12. What is the average length of four pieces of wood which measure 2.10m, 1.80m, 3.65m and 2.45m?

A	B	C	D	E
2.50m	2.75m	2.80m	2.85m	2.90m

Answer = ☐

13. A customer withdraws £240 from her account. She gets half the money in £20 notes and the remainder in £10 notes. How many notes does she receive?

A	B	C	D	E
12	15	18	20	24

Answer = ☐

14. How many 568ml cartons of milk are there in a chiller unit if the total quantity of milk being stored is 17. 040 litres?

A	B	C	D	E
20	25	30	34	35

Answer = ☐

15. If 3m of chain-fencing are needed to link up two posts, what is the total length required to link up ten posts?

A	B	C	D	E
20m	27m	30m	32m	36m

Answer = ☐

16. A constable leaves the house at 08.00 hours and returns at 17.30 hours. How many hours has she been away from home?

A	B	C	D	E
8	8½	8¾	9½	10

Answer = ☐

17. A car park is full and contains 150 cars. If 40 cars are blue, 30 are white and 30 are green and the rest are red, what percentage must be red?

A	B	C	D	E
25%	33.3%	50%	66.6%	70%

Answer = ☐

18. A street has 26 houses. Two houses receive five letters each, ten receive three each and the rest get one each. How many letters have been delivered in total?

A	B	C	D	E
38	44	48	52	54

Answer = ☐

19. Five parcels of equal weight cost £16.25 to send by post. What is the cost per parcel?

A	B	C	D	E
£3.10	£3.15	£3.25	£3.75	£3.95

Answer = ☐

20. One carpet tile measures 50cm by 50cm. How many tiles are required to cover a floor which measures 5m by 4m?

A	B	C	D	E
80	85	90	94	100

Answer = ☐

Test 2

1. If £15.43 is spent on leisure activities each week, how much is spent in eight weeks?

A	B	C	D	E
£105.72	£110.72	£115.52	£121.24	£123.44

   Answer = ☐

2. If one copy of a report weighs 140g, how much do 150 reports weigh?

A	B	C	D	E
19kg	20kg	21kg	22kg	23kg

   Answer = ☐

3. If a car journey of 325 miles takes 5 hours, what is the average speed of the car?

A	B	C	D	E
60mph	65mph	68mph	70mph	75mph

   Answer = B

4. The total takings for a single theatrical performance amounts to £1770. If one seat costs £6, how many people are in the audience?

A	B	C	D	E
255	260	275	295	300

   Answer = ☐

5. How many pieces of string, each measuring 1.5m, can be cut from a ball which is 90m long?

A	B	C	D	E
35	40	50	60	65

   Answer = ☐

6. If 70% of £350 has been spent, how much money remains?

A	B	C	D	E
£105	£110	£115	£120	£125

   Answer = ☐

7. An officer leaves home in his car at 07.30 hours and reaches his destination at 13.45. How long is it since he left his house?

A	B	C	D	E
6hrs	6¼hr	6½hr	7hr	7¼hr

Answer = ▢

8. If one ticket costs £4.20, how much will it cost for a party of nine?

A	B	C	D	E
£37.50	£37.80	£38.50	£39	£39.80

Answer = ▢

9. 25% of 180 people attending a function are smokers. How many are non-smokers?

A	B	C	D	E
45	75	90	130	135

Answer = ▢

10. The combined weekly wage packets for a family contain four £100 notes, three £50 notes, six £20 notes and five £1 coins. How much does the family earn in a week?

A	B	C	D	E
£575	£595	£655	£675	£685

Answer = ▢

11. If I begin an eight-hour shift at 08.30 and do one hour's overtime, what time will I finish work?

A	B	C	D	E
16.30	17.00	17.30	18.00	18.30

Answer = ▢

12. A room measures 6m by 4.5m and has two doorways each 90cm wide. What length of skirting board is required?

A	B	C	D	E
18.20m	19.20m	19.80m	20.20m	21.00m

Answer = ▢

13. If eight notepads cost £6.08, how much is the price of one pad?

A	B	C	D	E
76p	78p	80p	81p	82p

Answer = ☐

14. A printing machine produces 30 pages a minute. At this rate, how long will it take to print a 360-page document?

A	B	C	D	E
10min	12min	13min	15min	16min

Answer = ☐

15. A set meal in a restaurant costs £5.60. If senior citizens are given a 5% reduction, what would the bill amount to if ten senior citizens had such a meal?

A	B	C	D	E
£55.30	£54.20	£53.60	£53.20	£52.90

Answer = ☐

16. If braid costs 56p a metre, how much will 20m cost?

A	B	C	D	E
£12.12	£11.56	£11.20	£10.80	£10.56

Answer = ☐

17. Items totalling £260 were purchased by writing a cheque for £46 and adding £63 to a store account. How much cash was used to pay for the remaining amount?

A	B	C	D	E
£171	£165	£161	£155	£151

Answer = ☐

18. If I jog every day for 30 minutes, how much time do I spend jogging in seven days?

A	B	C	D	E
2½hr	2¾hr	3hr	3½hr	3¾hr

Answer = ☐

19. The garden shown below has two vegetable plots and a path 2m wide. What area of turf would be required to cover the plots?

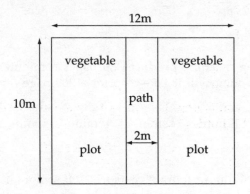

A	B	C	D	E
50m²	100m²	120m²	125m²	140m²

Answer = ☐

20. The petrol tank of a car has a maximum capacity of 48 litres. If the tank is a quarter full, how many litres of petrol are needed to fill it to maximum?

A	B	C	D	E
12	26	28	34	36

Answer = ☐

Test 3

1. If three accidents occur on average every two days at a crossroad, how many accidents will occur on average every eight days?

A	B	C	D	E
4	6	8	12	16

    Answer =

2. One case containing 12 bottles of wine costs £48. How much will 3 bottles cost?

A	B	C	D	E
£11	£12	£14	£16	£18

    Answer =

3. A health club raises its annual subscription of £240 by 15%. What will the new subscription cost?

A	B	C	D	E
£255	£260	£266	£276	£312

    Answer =

4. If I spend £1.50, £2.05 and £3.20 on items for lunch, how much have I spent in total?

A	B	C	D	E
£6.55	£6.65	£6.75	£6.85	£7.05

    Answer =

5. An investor withdraws 40% of her savings from an account which holds £800. How much remains in the account?

A	B	C	D	E
£480	£460	£420	£320	£310

    Answer =

6. A stolen wallet contains two £100 notes, seven £50 notes, three £10 notes and two £5 notes and 75p in coins. How much money has been stolen?

A	B	C	D	E
£555.75	£560.75	£570.75	£580.75	£590.75

    Answer =

7. If 20 pages of a 240 page notepad are used every day, how many days will it be until a replacement pad is needed?

A	B	C	D	E
6	10	11	12	13

    Answer = ☐

8. How much does it cost to buy 14 box files at £3.50 each?

A	B	C	D	E
£48.50	£49	£49.50	£50	£53.50

    Answer = ☐

9. What sum of money remains if I started with £25 in my wallet and I spent £13.36?

A	B	C	D	E
£10.64	£10.74	£11.64	£12.46	£12.64

    Answer = ☐

10. If I go on duty at 14.30 and finish at 22.30, how many hours will I have worked in five days?

A	B	C	D	E
30hr	35hr	40hr	42hr	44hr

    Answer = ☐

11. What is the total paved area of the garden shown below?

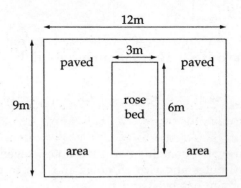

A	B	C	D	E
100m^2	90m^2	86m^2	82m^2	72m^2

Answer = ☐

12. What is the total weight of five packages each of 100g and six parcels each of 7.5kg?

A	B	C	D	E
36.5kg	40.5kg	42.5kg	45.5kg	50.5kg

Answer = ☐

13. If seven people gave taped interviews which lasted 1 hour 24 minutes in total, what was the length of one interview on average?

A	B	C	D	E
12min	13min	14min	15min	16min

Answer = ☐

14. If the number of season-ticket holders has fallen by ⅛ to 10,500, how many season-ticket holders have been lost?

A	B	C	D	E
1300	1400	1500	1650	1700

Answer = ☐

15. What is the average (mean) height of a group of people if two are 1.77m tall, three are 1.92m in height and one is 2.10m tall?

A	B	C	D	E
1.79m	1.81m	1.84m	1.87m	1.90m

Answer = ☐

16. A motorist is travelling at 56mph in a built-up area, where the speed limit is 30mph. By how much should the speed of the car be reduced to equal the speed limit?

A	B	C	D	E
17 mph	24 mph	26 mph	27 mph	28 mph

Answer = ☐

17. A box of decorations which cost £30 last Christmas is reduced in price by 12%. What is the revised price?

A	B	C	D	E
£25.40	£25.60	£26.40	£26.80	£26.90

Answer = ☐

18. A person who works a five-day week has been absent for 21 full days and 8 half days. How many weeks of work have been missed in total?

A	B	C	D	E
4	5	5.5	6	6.5

Answer = ☐

19. One vehicle in 15 is stopped in a traffic survey. How many vehicles will have been stopped out of 225?

A	B	C	D	E
11	12	13	14	15

Answer = ☐

20. If a drum can hold 120 litres of paraffin, how much will it cost to fill the empty drum when paraffin is priced at £1.99 for 4 litres?

A	B	C	D	E
£58.30	£58.60	£59.70	£59.90	£60.30

Answer = ☐

Answers to numerical reasoning tests

Test 1
(page 81)

1. = D
2. = E
3. = E
4. = B
5. = C
6. = D
7. = B
8. = C
9. = E
10. = D
11. = C
12. = A
13. = C
14. = C
15. = B
16. = D
17. = B
18. = E
19. = C
20. = A

Test 2
(page 85)

1. = E
2. = C
3. = B
4. = D
5. = D
6. = A
7. = B
8. = B
9. = E
10. = D
11. = C
12. = B
13. = A
14. = B
15. = D
16. = C
17. = E
18. = D
19. = B
20. = E

Test 3
(page 89)

1. = D
2. = B
3. = D
4. = C
5. = A
6. = E
7. = D
8. = B
9. = C
10. = C
11. = B
12. = D
13. = A
14. = C
15. = E
16. = C
17. = C
18. = B
19. = E
20. = C

Chapter 7

PIR4 Verbal Logical Reasoning Test

Introduction

In this test you are given a series of descriptions of situations which are typical of those encountered by police officers in the course of their duties, together with additional facts which are known about them. In each case they are followed by a number of conclusions which might be drawn from the information provided. Your task is to evaluate each of the conclusions in the light of the evidence given and then to decide if:

A   The conclusion is *true* given the situation described and the facts which are known about it.

B   The conclusion is *false* given the situation described and the facts which are known about it.

C   It is *impossible* to say whether the conclusion is true or false given the situation described and the facts which are known about it.

Now take a look at the example given on page 96. Read through the description of the situation and the facts known about it and then evaluate each of the five conclusions. Mark your answer A, B or C in the answer boxes provided.

    Four practice tests of this type are given below. Tests 1, 2 and 3 each consist of 20 questions. Allow yourself 15 minutes per test. Test 4 contains 40 questions which you should try to answer in 25 minutes. Work as quickly and as accurately as you can. If you are not sure of an answer, mark your best choice, but avoid wild guessing. If you want to change an answer, rub it out completely and then write your new answer in the box provided. Give yourself one mark for each correct answer and make a note of the scores to see if you are improving from one test to another. In this sub test in the real PIRT, you will be allowed 25 minutes to answer 40 questions.

Example

> Brian Jones aged 10 and Ben Wilson aged 12 were reported missing at 8pm on 9 May after they failed to return home from a cycle ride to some nearby woods. Police have set up a search party for the two missing boys. It is also known that:
>
> ● The woods are very dense and over 10 hectares in area.
> ● Two boys were admitted to a local hospital at 5pm.
> ● Brian Jones lived with his stepmother.
> ● Ben Wilson was an only child living with his father.
> ● Ben had a new 10 gear racing bike.
> ● The wood has several ponds and swampy areas.
> ● Brian was picked upon at school by the older students.
> ● Ben saw the educational psychologist at school each week.

1. The two boys could have run away from home. ☐

2. The boys had a cycling accident and were taken to hospital. ☐

3. Older students had picked on Brian in the woods. ☐

4. Ben had no brothers or sisters. ☐

5. Ben had no problems at school or home. ☐

Answers

1. = A   2. = C   3. = C   4. = A   5. = B

It should be pointed out that all of the names and situations in these verbal logical reasoning tests are fictitious and that any resemblance they bear to real persons, places, or events is purely coincidental.

Test 1

At 7.05pm on 12 December there was a loud explosion in Bathurst Street, house number 2. A woman and child managed to escape unhurt, but the ensuing fire claimed the lives of an elderly man and young baby. It is also known that:

- John Watts aged 91 owned 2 Bathurst Street.
- A smell of gas had been reported at 3pm on 12 December from 2 Bathurst Street.
- Fred Watts was informed of the death of his father John Watts and his baby George Watts, of 2 Bathurst Street, by the police at 8.30pm on 12 December.
- Fred Watts works nightshift at the local mine.
- Fred Watts is a divorcee.

---

1. The explosion at 2 Bathurst Street on 12 December was due to a leaking gas pipe. ☐

2. Fred Watts was married to the lady who escaped safely from the explosion. ☐

3. The police took less than two hours to find the house-owner's son. ☐

4. A gas leak could be the reason for the explosion. ☐

5. John Watts was not a grandfather. ☐

At 2.20am on Sunday, a four-wheel drive vehicle plunged over the edge of a steep mountain pass and burst into flames as it reached the valley bottom. There were no survivors. The sole victim has been identified as Mr John Joseph Broon of Muckty, a village 2 miles from the scene of the accident. It is also known that:

- John Broon was an alcoholic who sought help from Alcoholics Anonymous.
- John Broon had been at the local pub from 6pm on Monday to 2.10am on Tuesday.
- John Broon had a wife and two children.
- The barperson of the local pub had served John all night.
- The drive from the local pub to John's house took 15 minutes along a narrow twisty road which hugged the mountainside.
- A dead sheep was found on the valleyside, 100 metres from where the car had left the road.

6.   John Broon was on his way home when he was killed. ☐

7.   John Broon had swerved to miss a sheep on the narrow road and had gone over the edge of the valley. ☐

8.   John Broon was the only person in the car when it crashed. ☐

9.   The alcohol content of John Broon at 2.20am would have been over the legal limit. ☐

10.   John Broon had eaten a large supper at home with his wife and two children at 9pm on Monday. ☐

The new sports club at Dolchem was vandalised on Friday evening after the boy scouts had finished their weekly meeting in the new hall. Damages are expected to be over £4,000. It is also known that:

- The Parish Council was in debt after the construction of the new sports club.
- Local teenagers opposed the proposal to charge people to use the club's facilities.
- The boy scouts have abandoned the old village hall where they used to have meetings.
- There is a high level of youth unemployment in Dolchem.
- Witnesses saw a group of five youths running away from the club at 9.30pm on Friday.
- Spray cans were used on the club walls, liquid paint and faeces were deposited on the floor and windows were smashed.

11. Five young men were seen running away from the club at 9.30pm on Friday ☐

12. The boy scouts are willing to pay to use the new club. ☐

13. The youth of Dolchem had a motive to vandalise the new sports club. ☐

14. The Parish Council had profited from the construction of the new sports club. ☐

15. The idea of charging people to use the new sports facilities had caused some opposition among the younger members of the community. ☐

At 4.05pm on Sunday 3 June, an elderly man was found dead in Cuthbert Park. His right-hand wrist had been slashed. The park-keeper had seen a young man running out of the park at 3.30pm. The following facts are also known:

- The park had been shut for major landscape changes.
- The young man worked for the landscape contractors in the park.
- The dead man had been diagnosed with terminal cancer on Friday 1 June.
- The landscape contractors do not work on Sundays.
- The park-keeper is profoundly deaf.
- A sharp knife with a 16cm blade was found 100m from the dead body.
- The victim was right-handed.

16.   The park-keeper heard a scream from inside the park at 3.25pm on Sunday 3 June.   ☐

17.   The victim may have committed suicide.   ☐

18.   The young man running out of the park had just clocked off from his landscape work in the park.   ☐

19.   The knife had been used to slash the victim's wrist.   ☐

20.   The victim was mugged and stabbed by the young man.   ☐

Test 2

Joan Verse left her one-year-old daughter in the pram, outside the butcher's, as she went into the shop at 11.15am on Thursday 4 February. When she emerged, the pram and baby were not there. She rang the police and reported the theft of her daughter at 11.30am. A reliable witness saw a very tall, thin young man running down the street carrying a young baby at 11.20am that same morning. It is also known that:

- The butcher's shop is on a steep hill.
- Joan Verse was a divorcee with two children.
- It was extremely icy and temperatures were below freezing.
- Joan Verse was in the process of fighting for custody of her child against her ex-husband.
- Joan was 5ft 4in tall and her ex-husband was shorter than her and overweight.
- The pram was over 11 years old.
- Joan was having an affair with a college student.
- The street led to the village pond, 40m from the butcher's shop.

---

1. The baby girl had been kidnapped.   ☐

2. The college student may be the father of the one-year-old girl.   ☐

3. Joan's ex-husband was seen running down the street carrying a young baby on 4 February.   ☐

4. The pram brakes could have failed and the pram could have skidded down the street and across the frozen pond.   ☐

5. Joan Verse was a vegetarian.   ☐

On Saturday 12 May at 9.30am the groundsman at Dithcote Cricket Ground discovered that the wickets had been vandalised and the turf had been dug up and removed. The afternoon match between the Conservative Club and the Round Table had to be cancelled. By Sunday it was evident that weedkiller had been used on the pitch and had been spread in the shape of the CND symbol. It is also known that:

- The groundsman is in sole charge of entry into the grounds.
- The Borough of Dithcote was run by the Conservative Party.
- The local Conservative MP broke his leg on Thursday 10 May.
- The groundsman belongs to Greenpeace.
- The outside fence had been broken recently.
- A large campaign to make Dithcote a nuclear-free zone had recently failed to achieve its aim.
- Brian Agler is the local Conservative MP.
- Brian Agler had played county cricket.

6.   The Conservative Party had blocked the recent nuclear-free zone campaign in Dithcote. ☐

7.   The vandals may have broken into the cricket grounds. ☐

8.   Brian Agler was going to be the first batsman for the Conservative Club on Saturday 12 May. ☐

9.   The groundsman may have known the vandals. ☐

10.   Brian Agler is a right-wing extremist. ☐

A 17-year-old boy was found unconscious in his flat on 28 December at 11pm. He was taken immediately to hospital where his stomach was pumped. He regained consciousness but died shortly afterwards. Neighbours recall seeing various young people going into the flat at all hours of the day and night. Other facts known at this stage are:

- Peter Graick was a heroin addict.
- Empty bottles of spirits and paracetamol were found in the flat.
- Jo Hager supplied Peter with hard drugs.
- Peter used to frequent the local nightclub.
- Jo was the father of a two-month-old child.
- Jo's child was in care with AIDS.
- The victim was a compulsive gambler.
- The victim had bruises on his head.

11. The victim was homeless. □

12. Peter died of an overdose. □

13. Neighbours may have seen Jo Hager enter the flat. □□

14. The victim's child was in care. □

15. The neighbours took the victim to hospital. □

Between 12 March and 3 April there has been a number of cases of food poisoning at the old people's home. It has resulted in two deaths, permanent paralysis of one lady and continued hospitalisation for three other residents. The police are treating the cases as suspicious. It is also known that:

- The residents agree to leave 5% of their estate to the home on their death.
- The home is privately owned and run by ex-Major Johns.
- There has been a delay in the reporting of the food poisoning cases of at least 28 hours from the initial symptoms.
- Ex-Major Johns is a member of Alcoholics Anonymous.
- Janet Scree is the nurse in charge of the residents.
- Ex-Major Johns has trained as a pharmacist.
- The home is running at a loss.
- The chef ensures that the standards of hygiene in the kitchen are above the necessary level.
- Janet Scree is colour blind.

16. The poisoned residents were treated in the same hospital. ☐

17. Janet Scree may have muddled up the residents' medicines. ☐

18. The home will profit from the two deaths. ☐

19. The chef worked in hygienic conditions. ☐

20. The victims were taken to the hospital as soon as their symptoms developed. ☐

Test 3

A robbery was committed on 23 November at 10.10pm at a video shop. The robber had a small pistol. The robber made gruff noises but said no words. The robber left the shop and got into a car outside. The police later found an upturned car in a ditch 25 miles from the shop. It is also known that:

- Steven Tibbs crashed his car at 10.30pm on 23 November.
- The cashier was 6ft 2in tall.
- Mickson had recently lost his job at the video shop.
- The video shop usually had over £500 in the till.
- The robber was taller than the cashier.
- The cashier had a criminal record.
- Mickson was 5ft 6in tall.
- Davis drove the getaway car from the video shop.

1. The robber was a man. ☐

2. Steven Tibbs may be the robber. ☐

3. The cashier reported the robbery to the police. ☐

4. The robber could be a friend of the cashier. ☐

5. Mickson could be the robber. ☐

At 01.35 on Saturday 9 February a middle-aged man was rushed to Saint's hospital with serious face injuries. He is in a critical state in intensive care. Police are looking into the incident. The only other facts known at this stage are:

- There were 14cm of snow on the pavements in town.
- The victim was found outside a nightclub.
- The victim's face had been cut by glass.
- Three youths left the nightclub at midnight.
- The victim had been lying outside for over an hour before going to hospital.
- The hospital informed the police of the accident.
- The victim had no wallet or identification on him.
- Dennis Fraser was the only occupant in the intensive care unit at Saint's hospital on the morning of Saturday 9 February.

6. The police knew nothing about the accident until the hospital informed them. ☐

7. The victim was Dennis Fraser. ☐

8. The victim was drunk. ☐

9. The three youths may have robbed the victim. ☐

10. The victim left the nightclub at 01.05 on Saturday 9 February. ☐

A 13-year-old boy, Gareth Jones, was taken to Downston Police Station on Saturday 11 June under the suspicion of shoplifting. Gareth Jones denies all charges made against him. It is also known that:

- Gareth is an orphan.
- The shop detective has a grudge against Gareth because he is the best friend of his son.
- The shop video does not show Gareth on it.
- Gareth was caught stealing police bollards two years ago.
- The shop was extremely busy on Saturday 11 June.
- Gareth had not been given a receipt for the goods he had bought.
- Gareth was stopped after he had left the shop.

11. The police rang Gareth's mother to tell her where her son was. ☐

12. The shop detective had a motive for accusing Gareth. ☐

13. This was Gareth's first offence. ☐

14. Gareth had bought some goods. ☐

15. Gareth ran away on leaving the shop. ☐

Two masked gunmen held up the only bank in Tuisdale at 10.30am on Wednesday 23 May. They made a successful getaway with over £500,000. Police say that three men are helping them with their enquiries. It is also known that:

- Four people work at the bank.
- Six customers were in the bank at 10.30am.
- No shots were fired.
- Mrs Grainger left the bank at 10.28am on Wednesday 23 May.
- All the people in the bank were made to lie on the floor on their stomachs.
- Police chased the getaway car for 14 miles, then lost it.
- An alarm alerted the police to the hold-up.
- An orange Ford Escort drove away from the bank at high speed at 10.30am on Wednesday 23 May.

---

16. The gunmen fired a shot to make everyone lie down on the floor. ☐

17. The getaway car was an orange Ford Escort. ☐

18. The cashier pressed the alarm connected to the police station. ☐

19. At least six people were lying on the ground. ☐

20. Tuisdale's other bank provided access to cash for customers after the ordeal. ☐

Test 4

All the students at Risedale High School were sent home early on Tuesday 1 April 1990 due to a bomb scare in the science block. Police were called in after a brown parcel had been left unaccounted for in the physics laboratory. Bomb experts later revealed that it was a hoax. Police are treating the matter seriously. So far it is known that:

- John Dawes, an ex-pupil, was on school grounds on Tuesday 1 April.
- A group of sixth-form science students had been making minor explosives in the chemistry laboratory the previous week.
- The headteacher had recently made cuts in the science budget.
- The science staff opposed recent cuts and had threatened unreasonable behaviour.
- Joyce Denver (physics teacher) had bought a birthday present for her son before school on Tuesday 1 April.
- The school has a high truancy rate.
- Five pupils have been expelled since the start of the academic year.

1. The brown parcel was the birthday present of Joyce Denver's son. ☐

2. John Dawes had been expelled from Risedale School. ☐

3. The brown parcel could have been an April Fool's Day hoax. ☐

4. The school has had no other problems with students since September 1989. ☐

5. The science staff were free from suspicion. ☐

A 29-year-old man was found dead in his car at 3.25pm on Monday 7 August down a quiet country lane near Rulestone. Police said that the man had died of carbon monoxide poisoning. It is also known that:

- The victim, Giles Clark, was a recently appointed sales executive for an electrical firm, Viscox.
- Clark was found gagged and with his feet and hands tied.
- Clark had recently lost the company £¼ million worth of sales.
- The director of Viscox had recently been suspected of fraud.
- Two men of large build were seen walking a Rottweiler down the lane at 3.10pm on Monday 7 August.
- Clark had recently had his car in the garage.
- Clara, Clark's wife, had been having an affair with his work colleague, Charles Dence.

6. Two men of large build found Giles Clark's body in the car down the lane. ☐

7. Clark could have discovered his wife's affair and attempted suicide. ☐

8. Clark was a self-employed sales executive. ☐

9. Clark's car was in need of repair. ☐

10. Viscox had recently suffered a financial sales loss. ☐

A recent spate of money-extracting con-people has caused the police to issue warnings to elderly people not to let strangers into their homes. So far the police have the following facts to follow:

- Mrs Froode gave £63 to a young dark-haired man posing as an insurance broker.
- Mr Grace paid £29 to a smartly dressed 30-year-old woman who posed as a pension broker.
- The con-man who approached 27-year-old Ms Dodds was the driver of a BMW.
- Over 400 households had been contacted by a con-person within two days.
- All given addresses of supposed brokers have been found to be false.

11. The con-person was a transvestite. ☐

12. Several conmen and women were working together. ☐

13. Only old-age pensioners were approached. ☐

14. The con-people may have contacted people using the telephone. ☐

15. Potential victims all lived in a closely knit neighbourhood. ☐

Between 10 and 14 December, police have reported over 120 cases of sharp metal pieces being found in Janesons' mincemeat jars. Police have evidence to believe that the person responsible is an employee of Janesons. It is also known that:

- Janesons have rearranged their management structure and will be making 20 senior employees redundant in January.
- Ben Laidet was made redundant on 8 December for incompetent behaviour.
- Janesons' closest rival, Bertsons, have been suffering from severe financial losses since Janesons installed new technology in the bottling process, which increased output.
- Engineers recently overhauled the machinery.
- Janesons changed their dried fruit suppliers in November.
- The mincemeat is put into jars two weeks before going to the shops.
- The seals were unbroken on the contaminated jars.

16. Bertsons will benefit from Janesons' loss of custom.   ☐

17. Ben Laidet could have put the metal pieces in the mincemeat.   ☐

18. Metal may have come in from the new dried fruit suppliers.   ☐

19. The contaminated jars were probably bottled between 4 and 7 December.   ☐

20. Janesons had recently expanded their output.   ☐

A 36-year-old lady was hit and badly injured when a sportscar suddenly swerved off the road in the small village of Paddly. The lady was rushed immediately to Crownsby hospital at 12.45pm on Wednesday 3 October, where she is said to have reached a stable condition. A reliable witness said there seemed to be no obvious reason for the car to swerve so suddenly. The car did not stop and raced out of the village before police could follow. It is also known that:

- The victim was Jane Solled.
- Jane worked for an accountancy firm called Sayerston.
- The manager, Mr Sayerston, collected old sportscars.
- Jane had the day off on Wednesday 3 October.
- Jane had found copies of letters in the office which indicated fraudulent behaviour by someone in the firm.
- Mr Sayerston plays golf every Wednesday afternoon.
- Jane's father is a renowned barrister in Crownsby.
- At 1.05pm a young cyclist was admitted to Crownsby hospital with severe head injuries after being knocked off his bicycle.

21. Jane Solled was an accountant. ☐

22. Jane Solled was hit by a car while on her lunch hour from work. ☐

23. A car had knocked a young cyclist off his bicycle just after Jane's accident. ☐

24. Mr Sayerston was afraid of Jane's father. ☐

25. Crownsby hospital dealt with at least two road accident victims on Wednesday 3 October. ☐

On the evening of 3 November a mother and daughter were found dead in their two-bedroomed flat in Diswich. Both victims had suffocated and the police were treating the incident as suspicious. It is also known that:

- The victims were Mary Cauld, aged 24 years, and Sarah Cauld, aged 6 years.
- Mary Cauld's father had recently been released from prison.
- Sarah Cauld had been revealed HIV positive on 26 October.
- Gary Davison was Mary's ex-husband.
- A young man was seen near the flat on 2 November.
- The flat had not been broken into.
- Gary reported the deaths to the police at 6.45pm on 3 November.
- Mary Cauld was owed £900 by Gary and had threatened to take him to court if he didn't pay up soon.

26. Mary could have killed her own daughter. ☐

27. Gary Davison is an AIDS carrier. ☐

28. Mary's father was near the flat on 2 November. ☐

29. Sarah Cauld was a perfectly healthy child when she died. ☐

30. Gary was first to find the two dead bodies. ☐

Two inter-city train carriages were found ablaze last night (10 March) on a siding at Glundal railway station where they were awaiting repairs. Three elderly men were seen at the station at 7pm last night and reliable witnesses say they were all over 6ft tall and one man had a bad limp. It is also known that:

- Fred Wish is 6ft 5in tall and 58 years old.
- Bob Tuck is a retired train driver.
- Rod Debbs was made redundant by BR in January.
- The carriages had been taken out of service due to electrical faults.
- A violent thunderstorm occurred over Glundal on 10 March.
- John Plum is 64 years old and has just left hospital after a cartilage operation.
- 61-year-old Dennis White, an ex-BR worker, is 5ft 6in tall.

31. Rod Debbs had a motive for the arson attack.   ☐

32. Lightning could have started the fire.   ☐

33. Dennis White was one of the three elderly men.   ☐

34. Fred Wish could have been one of the three men at the station.   ☐

35. Bob Tuck is over 65 years old.   ☐

An eminent professor in chemistry was found in possession of unidentified human body parts, stored in his study. Fellow colleagues recall the professor's obsessive research projects of the last year and called the police when the professor's daughter-in-law went missing. It is also known that:

- The professor hadn't spoken to his son for two years after an argument.
- The daughter-in-law visited the professor at the university on a regular basis.
- The professor was a loner who worked all hours in his study.
- The professor had spent a year in a rehabilitation centre.
- The professor's present project is concerned with the storage of body organs.

36. The professor was once an alcoholic. ☐

37. The professor enjoyed the company of his daughter-in-law. ☐

38. The professor had been working hard all year on research projects. ☐

39. The professor could have killed his daughter-in-law for experimental reasons. ☐

40. The son was the only one who called in the police when his wife went missing. ☐

26/40

Answers to verbal logical reasoning tests

Test 1 (p 97)	Test 2 (p 101)	Test 3 (p 105)	Test 4 (p 109)
1. C	1. C	1. C	1. C
2. C	2. A	2. A	2. C
3. A	3. B	3. C	3. A
4. A	4. A	4. A	4. B
5. B	5. C	5. B	5. C
6. C	6. C	6. C	6. C
7. C	7. A	7. A	7. A
8. A	8. B	8. C	8. B
9. C	9. A	9. A	9. C
10. B	10. C	10. B	10. A
11. C	11. B	11. B	11. C
12. C	12. C	12. A	12. C
13. C	13. A	13. B	13. B
14. B	14. C	14. A	14. A
15. A	15. C	15. C	15. C
16. B	16. C	16. B	16. C
17. A	17. A	17. C	17. B
18. B	18. C	18. C	18. A
19. C	19. A	19. A	19. B
20. C	20. B	20. B	20. A
			21. C
			22. B
			23. C
			24. C
			25. A
			26. A
			27. C
			28. C
			29. B
			30. C
			31. C
			32. A
			33. B
			34. A
			35. C
			36. C
			37. C
			38. A
			39. A
			40. B

Chapter 8

PIR5 Observation Test

In this test you will be shown a series of scenes on a television screen followed by a number of questions which also appear on the screen. It is not possible, therefore, to provide you with practice tests in the same way as we have with those which simply use pencil and paper. What we intend to do instead, therefore, is to give you guidance on the observation test itself; and to suggest ways in which you can prepare for it.

The observation test

The aim of the observation test is to assess your ability to observe and recall information from real-life incidents which you have witnessed. Each of the scenes is shown only once and the questions appear on the screen as follows:

1	How many people were standing at the bus stop?
A	Three
B	Four
C	Five
D	Seven

Shortly after one question disappears from the screen it is replaced by another. A warning tone sounds every time the question on the screen changes. Since there is no chance for you to see either the scene or the questions again, you have to be alert and observant all of the time, otherwise you will miss vital clues and fail to make a mental note of crucial pieces of information.

In this test there is only one correct answer per question, so if you are not certain of your answer, the advice is to record your best choice on the mark sheet by filling in the appropriate space. However, as in all multiple-choice tests, you should try to avoid resorting to wild guessing.

The test itself lasts 25 minutes and consists of seven scenes, each of which is followed by seven questions, giving a total of 49 questions. The scenes depict incidents in which some criminal activity may have taken place. Hence the ability of a witness to observe and recall information accurately may be crucial to the police in the pursuit of an enquiry and in presenting evidence in a court of law. In the observation test, as a potential police officer, you become that witness.

How to prepare for the observation test

Some people may appear to be naturally more observant than others. They seem to be able to notice things which other people miss, and to be able to remember significant details long after the event. In court they are the sort of people who make good witnesses. In the police force their observation skills are invaluable in the day-to-day fight against crime. You may be lucky enough to be such a person, but if you are not, do not despair. As with other skills, systematic practice should help you to improve. However, before suggesting some practical activities which will help to develop the relevant skills, here is some further guidance on the observation test itself. Fundamentally, the observation test is about:

● sequences of events;
● the settings in which they occur;
● the people and objects involved in those events.

Put simply, sequences of events refer to the order in which things happen, for example:

● a person approaches a car, opens the boot, puts in a bag, closes the boot, unlocks the car door, gets in, starts the engine and then drives away;
● a bus stops, the automatic door opens, two passengers get off, six people get on, the door closes and the bus moves off.

Unfortunately, everyday sequences of events such as these can become so familiar to us that we no longer observe them carefully. As a result, we often assume that something has happened when that is not the case. So make a habit of noticing regular routines and patterns of behaviour in commonplace locations such as the ones listed below. The ability to recall the precise order in which things happened is a crucial element in observation skills including those actions and behaviours which look suspicious – for example, because they are unusual, atypical or out of sequence.

The settings are the places in which the observed sequences of events occurred. These are all commonplace locations with which you should be familiar, for example:

- car parks, railway stations and bus stops;
- outside corner shops, pubs and office blocks;
- suburban streets, housing estates and local parks.

They are, in fact, the places where a vigilant police officer might observe something which subsequently proves to be important. Details of the setting which might help to locate the place accurately include those in the:

- foreground: the features and objects which are near, such as the name of a shop or the number on a passing bus;
- background: landmarks in the far distance, such as the top of a tower block or the summit of a hill;
- middleground: the features which can be observed in the middle distance – that is, in between those which are near to you and those in the far distance, such as a railway bridge over the road or a public building at the end of the street.

The people are the 'actors' in the sequences of events which make up the incidents which you observe. Hence you must learn to take note of:

- how many people were involved, how old they were and what their gender was;
- how they were dressed – that is, distinctive colours, styles, hats – and how they behaved.

The objects are the inanimate things involved in the events observed. Hence you must learn to take note of such details as:

- motor vehicle registration numbers, colours, styles – for example, saloon or hatchback, makes, bodywork damage;
- briefcases or packages passed from one person to another.

You can begin to practise your observation skills at first hand for short intervals in everyday settings, such as the ones listed above. Try to behave naturally – you don't want some observant member of a Neighbourhood Watch scheme ringing the police because they think that you might be about to break into the house next door! Concentrate on a short sequence of events lasting no more than two minutes, together with details of the setting and the people and objects involved. Then write a short account (as if you were a police witness making a statement) describing what you have observed. When it is finished, ask someone to read it and then to question you about it with a view to identifying any gaps and inconsistencies in your observations. As in the PIRT, the questions they ask should focus on the events; the settings in which they occurred and, the people and the objects involved.

Alternatively, you could get someone to make a visual record of a sequence of events by means of photographs and allow you look at them for a couple of minutes. They should then take the photographs away and ask you some questions to test your ability to recall significant details. You could repeat the exercises described above using a video camera to record some sequences of events and a video playback system to show them to you on a television screen. Carefully chosen video recordings from broadcast television programmes could also be used in the same way. Finally, another way to sharpen up your observation skills is to do some 'before and after' exercises, for which you will need a partner. Get your partner to arrange about 20 everyday objects on a table; you study them for one minute and leave the room; your partner rearranges them and you have one minute to spot the differences. Alternatively, your partner makes some minor changes to a room with which you are familiar and you have to identify the differences.

Further Reading from Kogan Page

Great Answers to Tough Interview Questions, 3rd edition, Martin John Yate, 1992

How to Pass Computer Selection Tests, Sanjay Modha, 1994

How to Pass Graduate Recruitment Tests, Mike Bryon, 1994

How to Pass Selection Tests, Mike Bryon and Sanjay Modha, 1991

How to Pass Technical Selection Tests, Mike Bryon and Sanjay Modha, 1993

How to Pass the Civil Service Qualifying Tests, Mike Bryon, 1995

How to Pass Numeracy Tests, Harry Tolley and Ken Thomas 1996

How to Pass Verbal Reasoning Tests, Harry Tolley and Ken Thomas, 1996

Interviews Made Easy, Mark Parkinson, 1994

Test Your Own Aptitude, 2nd edition, Jim Barrett and Geoff Williams, 1990